A
Human
Search

A
Human
Search

BEDE GRIFFITHS
REFLECTS ON HIS LIFE

AN ORAL HISTORY
Edited by John Swindells

TRIUMPH™ BOOKS
Liguori, Missouri

Published by Triumph™ Books
Liguori, Missouri
An Imprint of Liguori Publications

Most photographs courtesy of the family of David Griffiths, as well as Fr. Christudas and the library of Saccidananda Ashram.

Library of Congress Cataloging-in-Publication Data
Griffiths, Bede, 1906-1993
    A human search : Bede Griffiths reflects on his life / edited by
John Swindells. – 1st ed.
        p.   cm.
    ISBN 0-89243-935-1
    1. Griffiths, Bede, 1906-1993. 2. Benedictines–Biography.
3. Catholic Church–England–Clergy–Biography. 4. Catholic Church –
India–Clergy–Biography. 5. Spiritual biography–England.
6. Spiritual biography–India.   I. Swindells, John.   II. Title.
    BX4705.G5133A3   1996
    271'.102
    [B]–dc20   96-14512
                                                           CIP

Printed in the United States of America
01 00 99 98 97   5 4 3 2 1

First Edition

Contents

+≒⇒+

Acknowledgments   vii

List of Illustrations   viii

Foreword   ix

Introduction   xix

1. The Early Years   1

2. The Shaping of the Mind — College Days   19

3. Eastington — An Experiment in Communal Life   37

4. The Dark Night   49

5. Catholicism and Benedictine Life   55

6. The Journey to India   67

7. The Stroke — Discovering the Feminine   87

8. Science and Religion   105

9. Seasoned Thoughts   113

10. The Reflections of Others   131

Appendix: History and Interpretation of the Bible   147

Acknowledgments

I would like to thank the following for their assistance without whom this film and book would not be possible:

My coproducer and friend Robin Wood, who shared the vision for this project and appreciated Father Bede's important contribution to the world; Kennedy Wood, for his generosity and support; Andrew Harvey, for his passion, knowledge, and enthusiasm; Fr. Christudas, Sister Marie Louise, and the residents and staff at Saccidananda Ashram, for their love and trust; Fr. Douglas Conlan, for his generosity and support; Nicole Alchen, for her many painstaking hours of transcription; Laura Zusters, Tony Gailey, and Rob Stalder, for their wonderful filmmaking abilities; Roland and Christiane Ropers, for their friendship and support; Fr. Patrick Eastman, for his review of the manuscript and helpful suggestions; Joseph Kulin at *Parabola,* for his kindness and belief in this work; and Patricia Kossmann at Triumph Books, for her tenacity and editing genius.

LIST OF ILLUSTRATIONS

Frontispiece: Fr. Bede outside Kurisumala Ashram during the 1980s.

Introduction: Fr. Bede and Members of the Film Crew during the filming of the documentary, "A Human Search," 1992.

Fr. Bede feeding local villagers at his Ashram during the late 1980s.

Chapter 1: Fr. Bede (Alan Richard Griffiths) as a young child with his mother, Harriet Lillian Griffiths, in England, approximately 1910.

Chapter 2: Fr. Bede as a young man in England, possibly during his Oxford days, early 1920s.

Fr. Bede with relatives or a friend's family during his Oxford days. Alan is the second from left.

Chapter 3: Cottages in the Cotswolds in the English countryside where Bede and his friends retreated after graduating from Oxford.

Chapter 4: Returning to ordinary life, Bede struggles for discernment.

Chapter 5: Fr. Bede during his time at Prinknash Abbey; and in the garden of the monastery with a visitor (probably his friend Martyn Skinner), in the 1930s.

Chapter 6: The ship that took Fr. Bede and Benedict Alapatt to India in 1955.

Bede aboard ship with Alapatt and a female friend, Dr. Allan, who paid for his fare.

Chapter 7: Fr. Bede before his final stroke, in 1992.

Chapter 8: Fr. Bede conducting a ritual baptism on one of his birthdays during the 1980s at the River Cauvery next to Saccidananda Ashram.

Fr. Bede celebrating evening Mass at Saccidananda Ashram, early 1992.

Chapter 9: Fr. Bede discussing a text with an Ashram guest during the 1970s.

Chapter 10: Fr. Bede with His Holiness, The Dalai Lama of Tibet, and Fr. Douglas Conlan, in Perth, Australia, 1992.

Appendix: Fr. Bede speaking in Sydney, Australia, in 1985.

Foreword

Dom Bede Griffiths, OSB Cam.: A Personal Remembrance

Bede Griffiths first came into my life when I was a teenager growing up in Hartford, Connecticut. In Hartford — the insurance capital of the world — there is a very modern cathedral dedicated to and named after Saint Joseph. To me, the cathedral looks like a huge bathtub, and I've always thought of it in that way. I've never liked it because it's such a cold-looking place, but it provided the environment for my spiritual life as a teenager and young adult. The pastor, Monsignor John S. Kennedy, a well-known writer, went to great lengths to assure our literacy by installing a large rack of books in the back of the church with more than a hundred titles. In those days, my income was a modest allowance, and on one particular day, as I was coming from mass, I spied the image of a very slender, aseptic-looking man in a white habit on the cover of an Image paperback. The title was celebrated, *The Golden String*, and it was the autobiography of Father Bede. Immediately I knew I must have this book, but I had only a dime in my pocket, and the book was around $1.50. There was just one copy of it. So I put the dime in the "donation" box and took the book.

I read it completely and enjoyed it thoroughly, though I'm not sure I understood it all. Some of it required a philosophical background, which I lacked at the time. *The Golden String* — a title suggested by Blake's poem — is really a kind of phenomenology of faith; that is, it describes with eloquence and maturity of insight the unfolding of faith for a person whose mind remained open in the midst of a vague sort of agnosticism. This agnosticism was resolved only at Oxford, when C. S. Lewis, who became a lifelong friend, was Father Bede's tutor. Lewis was also vaguely agnostic, but together they rediscovered their Christian faith.

I had eagerly read Bede's autobiography and then forgot it. Several years later, while I was teaching basic studies, comparative religion, anthropology, and sociology on a high school level in Hartford, a friend of mine returned from India after having spent two long periods with Bede at his ashram in South India, Shantivanam. My friend was an Olivetian Benedictine monk at the time (we had previously attended St. Anselm College in Manchester, New Hampshire, an institution run by the Benedictines, a kind of Catholic Dartmouth). His name was Bernard Peters, now Francis Peters. Bernard taught alongside me in Hartford, and during the lunch periods we would talk endlessly of India and Father Bede. It greatly stirred my heart and my curiosity. I had many questions. He suggested one day that I write to Father Bede, and I did so in 1973.

A long correspondence ensued. Bede was always at me to come to India, and I always found a reason not to go. Though I wanted to make the journey to the East, I was a little apprehensive of taking the plunge. After all, there are snakes and scorpions on the subcontinent. Besides which, I had responsibilities that kept me from going. It was not until the summer of 1979 that Father Bede and I met for the first time. He was coming to the States, and he wrote to me about it. At that time I was in graduate school at Fordham University in the Bronx. Bede came into America in New York City — having been here one time before in 1963 — and I met him at Kennedy Airport with a friend, Robert Fastiggi, a fellow graduate student at Fordham.

The moment I saw Bede, I knew he was a special being, a teacher and a friend. I've had three other such people in my life: a saintly uncle, John Cosgrove, Sister Mary Sarah, a Mercy sister who was my Latin professor, and Father Thomas Keating, a Trappist spiritual teacher and contemplative master. When I saw Bede, something leaped in my soul. He was no ordinary mortal. In 1979 he was in better health, and he had more energy. He looked like a biblical figure, or a desert father, with his long hair and beard. He was terribly thin, and someone had remarked to me that Father Bede didn't eat enough to sustain a cockroach, something that later, in India, I learned was untrue. What I noticed about him from the very beginning was a marvelous quality of openness, an enthusiasm, and a spontaneity. I was immediately drawn to him. When he'd speak, he would forget himself, or transcend self-consciousness, and a wonderful thing would always happen. The Divine Presence would radiate and stream forth from his luminous blue-gray eyes. I was amazed and inspired, and so I followed him. I spent much time with him that summer in America and England, then again in the summer of 1983, then in India in 1986, 1987, 1988, and 1989. In 1990, 1991, and 1992 he came here again.

The primary reason for these subsequent visits to America was to spend months at a time with a small group of us doing an experiment in contemplative living. Our group included Russill Paul D'Silva and his wife, Asha Paul, Father Bede, and myself. Russill and Asha were Bede's closest disciples, and Russill had himself been a monk in Bede's monastic ashram. At other times, and for brief periods, we were joined by Sister Pascaline Coff, a Benedictine, Father Thomas Keating, Father Laurence Freeman, an English Benedictine, Eusebia D'Silva, a Canadian, Sivaraj Sivanandam, an Indian, and Mark Brody, a psychologist from Wayne, Pennsylvania.

Two of these periods were spent in Waitsfield, Vermont, in a rugged but substantial house on eighty acres at the base of a mountain. The house belongs to Harrison Hobletzelle — Hob, as he is called by his friends — and his wife, Olivia, and they trek there to get away from Boston. Hob joined us often during the first stay in 1990, when Olivia was away in India, and she joined us the second time, when Hob's back had given out and he was unable to make the four-hour trip to Waitsfield. These times were from September to December 1990, and for six weeks during the summer of 1992, while the other times were in Oakland, California, and at Osage Monastery in Sand Springs, Oklahoma, Sister Pascaline's community. These were extraordinary times of happiness with Bedeji, as we called him affectionately.

We knew Bede the person, the simple, radiant, loving presence, the human Bede. At Waitsfield he was not, to us, the public figure, but one of us, living the contemplative life amid the splendors of nature, the rhythm of day and night, of morning stillness and evening mystery. We would rise around 5:30 A.M. and have morning prayer after tea or coffee. The prayer would also include a half hour of meditation, sometimes as much as forty minutes. Then we would enjoy breakfast in silence. After breakfast we'd quickly do the dishes while Bede looked on, though he'd often assist at the noon and evening dishes. After breakfast cleanup we'd sit with Bede for a half hour of *satsang,* or keeping company with the wise. From 9:00 A.M. to 12:00 noon we had time for work or study. Bede would read or write letters during this time. He was a great correspondent and would sometimes write as many as twenty letters a day! We took turns cooking, and I always looked forward to Russill and Asha's preparations because they were always some Indian dish, excellent beyond imagining.

During lunch we also kept silence while someone read, an old monastic custom. When the dishes were cleared away and cleaned, we all retired for a nap of about an hour. This nap was very important for Father Bede's health, and we guarded it for him. We also enjoyed the luxury of being able to take a needed rest period. Bede's health, which had been tenuous when we came, gradually improved with the tender care of Asha, Russill, and myself, not to mention the controlled diet, rest, and a stressless environment. His cheeks had a blush of color from the rest, the mountain air, and his vigorous walks. Each day he'd walk about forty minutes, covering nearly two miles, and this was someone who was then eighty!

We would have evening prayer and meditation around 5:00 P.M., followed by dinner. Oftentimes we'd engage in conversation during the evening meal, which would then spill over into the time for cleanup and recreation. Our evenings were likewise simple affairs. Russill, who is quite a musical genius, would take out his musical instruments, and play/sing one of his latest pieces. He also gave three or four concerts to a larger gathering during our two stays in Waitsfield. We had many good laughs together, told jokes, and recited poetry, a favorite pastime of Bede, who had committed to memory numerous poems from the English Romantic tradition. He and Hob would take turns reciting a celebrated poem.

One humorous incident took place during our first stay in Waitsfield. Russill, Asha, and I were night owls compared to Bede, who retired each evening around 9:00 P.M. We'd stay up to 11:30, or even 1:00. One time we were up a bit after 12:00, and we knew Bede would wake at 5:00 requesting a cup of tea. When we were getting ready for bed after midnight, we saw that Bede was still awake. So, while Asha and I kept Bede busy, Russill crawled under the bed and turned the clock back an hour. Bede never knew the difference, though he awoke at 4:00 A.M. Eventually, we owned up to the ruse, and we laughed about this long and hard.

Bede Griffiths was many things: church critic, synthesizer, prophet, icon, mystic, visionary, and theological iconoclast. Those of us who read *The Tablet,* London's Catholic weekly, are familiar with Bede's famous letters to the editor. Whenever he had something to say about the Vatican, or what he regarded as abuse of papal or church authority, he would write a strong letter to *The Tablet.* John Wilkins, the editor, had confided to me that he often had to tone down Bede's letters since they were so powerfully expressed, and Archbishop Rembert Weakland, who called Bede in Vermont during our first stay, told him how much he enjoyed his letters in *The Tablet!*

At the same time Bede was also quite capable of seeing implications of new developments in science, especially in physics, cosmology, biology, and psychology. He really had a genius for synthesis, much like that of Thomas Aquinas. He saw that the new science is compatible with mystical spirituality, and this was a constant theme of his for several years, culminating in a book, *A New Vision of Reality: Western Science, Eastern Mysticism, and Christian Faith* (Springfield, IL: Templegate, 1990). No less than Rupert Sheldrake, the British biologist and a great friend of Bede's, having written his first book, *The New Science of Life,* at Shantivanam, speaks of the emerging congeniality between science and religion, or contemplative spirituality.

Bede was also very much a prophetic figure, pointing the way for the Church, society, and the world. He saw Christianity, for instance, not in isolation, but in dynamic relationship with all the other world religions. That relationship he characterized as one of complementarity: the religions completing one another. It can be said that this relationship is one existing within the context of community, that community is the new model through which the various religions can come together. He perceived the Church's task to be that of assimilation of the spiritual wisdom of the Asian traditions, the Native American, the African, etc., just as it once had done in relation to Greco-Roman culture and philosophy.

It is also true to say that this simple English *Sannyasi,* or renunciate, as monks are called in India, is a kind of icon, and this iconic function has two meanings. First, he is an icon of reversal because in his great humility in deciding to set out for India in 1955 to, as he wrote to a friend at the time, "seek the other half of my soul," his mystical, intuitive, feminine half, Bede had actually reversed history in himself. He came to India as a docile student of India's immense spiritual and psychological wisdom, not as the British Empire had come two centuries before, as a conqueror. His mentality slowly was transformed into an authentically Indian one, although he retained his impeccable English breeding and education. Second, the term icon also suggests a symbol, a bridge symbol, as Judson Trapnell points out in his writings on Bede.* I would put it more strongly and say Bede is an existential symbol, a new identity of the Christian expanding beyond the cultural limitations of a Euro-centric theology and spirituality. Bede is totally universal without compromising the Christian faith.

My long experience and observation of Father Bede has convinced me of his inner mystical life, that Bede was indeed a mystic. I don't believe his mystical process was as developed as, say, that of Thomas Keating, but certainly more than that of Thomas Merton. It is true that his later stroke, and the inner explosion of mystical consciousness that emerged in early 1990, represent an advanced stage of contemplation. Bede's words about his experience on his last day at school before going up to Oxford indicate that he had had an awakening in the midst of nature, or an experience of the nature mysticism type. He also spoke from time to time about other encounters with the Divine. One involved

---

*See especially his "Bede Griffiths' Theory of Religious Symbol and Practice of Dialogue" (Washington: Catholic University, unpublished doctoral dissertation, 1993).

praying all night on his knees, during which he achieved another state of awareness, though he remembered little of its content. Then in 1990, after his stroke, when he began to experience the feminine, he wrote a letter to me in which he said: "I find myself in the Void, but the Void is totally saturated with Love." I have often thought and said that with this statement his inner experience traversed two mystical traditions, the Buddhist and the Christian.

Bede was also quite a visionary, and this characteristic is related to all of the above, and to his often theological iconoclasm. He realized that the world, or the global order of nation states, churches, societies, corporations, and institutions, had to change because they were stuck in the past, and engaged in a relentless, irresponsible, irrepressible consumption of the earth's resources, usually in a systemically unjust manner. He exhorted simplicity of life and community, and I remember his reaction after visiting the United Nations, where he spent a few hours with Dr. Robert Muller, who was then the assistant secretary general for Inter-Agency Affairs at the UN. Upon leaving the UN, Bede turned and said: "The renewal of the world will not come through that organization. It has to come from the earth itself, something much more basic." His theological iconoclasm was not a destructive exercise, but an attempt to stretch categories and to find new ways to express the Christian mystery in the Indian context, and in all other cultures that are not Western. His many lectures and articles on this topic encourage the development of an Indian Christian theology that is, as he oftentimes remarked, "thoroughly Indian and thoroughly Christian."

It is my firm and growing conviction that Bede Griffiths's

influence will steadily expand, and will come to radiate the third millennium like a brilliant supernova. John Swindells's book is an important contribution to Bedean studies because it presents Bede's rich life in his own words and through the impressions of others, most of whom knew him well. The book, though a transcription of John's film on Bede, allows the reader the leisure to pause and ponder Bedeji's own descriptions of, and insights into, his life and mystical depth. It is a wonderful book that makes Bede humanly accessible to the ages that come after him. Its value is greatly increased since the film itself was taken a few days prior to Bede's stroke in December 1992, and the more devastating one of January 1993. We must all thank John for this precious service.

WAYNE TEASDALE
Chicago, December 7, 1996

Introduction

HAVING BEEN what could possibly be described as an eclectic agnostic with mystical sympathies, I still find it quite extraordinary that I would have taken a film crew to India to document the life of a Christian Benedictine monk.

Belonging to a generation that grew up to be cynical of religious dogma and institutional intentions, I had very little time for organized religion. I would often defer to scientific rationalism to find answers to puzzling questions; and if there remained any doubts, I would become very busy, finding distractions from my concerns.

In my late twenties, in my own search for meaning, I began to meditate. This brought about a chain of events that led me to Bede Griffiths and has continued to lead me on to other extraordinary individuals and experiences.

Meditation took me within myself, and into a different sense of time and space. This led me into a very different perception of the world. In the process I seem to have found a new perspective regarding external concerns and have developed an understanding of my own center and quest for spiritual balance.

My perception of people also changed. I began to notice that some people were more content, serene, perhaps even more centered than the average, and I became curious as to why they were like this and how they came to be so.

As fate would have it, in 1992 I wound up working on the Australian tour of His Holiness the Dalai Lama of Tibet, and had the great privilege of meeting this profoundly simple man. I had never met anyone so clear and consistent, intelligent and wise, and at the same time so gentle and compassionate. On reflection, I felt no infatuation, no desire to run off and enter an ashram or follow a guru. I just felt that I had encountered someone with extraordinary integrity and presence. I felt enriched and inspired.

Several days later, while unwinding from this experience, I was casually reading through the *Sydney Morning Herald* and came across a large photograph of another extraordinary character — this time an old Western man with a long white beard, wearing the *kavi* (the robes of an Eastern holy man). He was sitting under a tree and looked like the archetypal wise old man of myth and legend. In fact, he looked a bit like Merlin, but at the same time he looked incredibly holy. The caption read, "East Meets West in the Venerable Bede." I was fascinated.

I picked up the phone and called the newspaper to find out if they had any more information about Father Bede's public engagements, but they were unable to help me. After making several other calls, I contacted the Adyar Bookshop, Sydney's religious and spiritual bookstore, to find out if they had any of Father Bede's books.

The clerk told me that they had three of his works in stock, and I asked that he hold them for me. Then I asked whether he knew where Father Bede would be appearing in Sydney. He then informed me that Father Bede had just walked into the store. What makes this synchronicity even more astounding is that Father Bede, considering he was eighty-five at the time and quite frail, was unlikely to be running around Sydney on a shopping spree.

Several days later I found myself with a friend, Robin Wood, in a civic hall in Sydney's northern suburbs awaiting the arrival of Father Bede. A tall, frail old man dressed in saffron robes with well-groomed long silver hair and beard took the stage. I knew, once again, I was in the presence of someone extraordinary. He began to speak in a kind, gentle voice, with a fine Oxford English accent. I was overwhelmed with a sense of mission and urgency. I turned to Robin and told her that I had to document this man's journey and try to capture some of his grace on film so that others could appreciate him after he was gone. I sat through his wise yet delicate oration for the next hour, preoccupied with trying to figure out how this would come about.

We were unable to meet Father Bede personally that evening. In fact, I didn't meet him until we arrived at his ashram ready to shoot the film months later. I had written to him immediately to request his permission to film the documentary and proceed with trying to raise the necessary funds. His response to my letter was positive, though precise and brief. He had agreed to the film being made.

Over the next few months I read everything I could find that Bede had written and that had been written about him. I proceeded to write a treatment for a one-hour documentary film, with the intention of raising funds to go into production. Father Bede's advanced age and frail health made it very difficult to proceed through the normal fund-raising and marketing channels. The odds were against his living much longer. As film is very much a money game, this constituted a bad risk for conventional players. My own limited experience as a filmmaker, combined with the fact that we would be shooting on location in India, issued an enormous challenge.

My enthusiasm must have been infectious, because by now Robin had agreed to coproduce the film with me, and a private investor agreed to put up the funds necessary to take a small crew to India. Within five months of discovering Father Bede in the newspaper, I was walking through the front gates of Saccidananda Ashram, Bede's home in southern India.

Our Australian crew included a very talented but very laconic cameraman who began to wonder what he had gotten himself into, uttering very dry one-liners throughout the shoot. Our sound recordist was a little less wary, and took the whole thing in stride, while our production manager got down to practicalities and set out to make the most of the basic accommodations and facilities that greeted us.

My role was that of facilitator. I assembled a team that would best assist Father Bede in articulating his story on film. In addition to our production crew, I had already secured the services of an experienced and very talented editor in Sydney before we departed.

Very insecure about my ability to ask the right questions, I sought the assistance of an old friend and expert on all things mystical, Andrew Harvey. Also an accomplished poet, novelist, and academic, Andrew would provide a depth and range of knowledge that I could not even aspire to. Following a number of communications by phone and fax, Andrew and I met in Mahabalipurram, just south of Madras. I had flown in from Sydney, he from Paris. Robin would arrive a week later with the equipment and crew. Andrew and I had decided to meet up the week before their arrival in order to review the script and prepare for our series of interviews with Father Bede.

Nothing had prepared me for India. I had considered myself reasonably well traveled, having covered most of Australia, North America, Southeast Asia, and Europe. Andrew, who is actually Anglo-Indian, had spent much of his childhood in southern India. But for me, India was a revelation — unlike anything I had experienced before. I became immediately intoxicated by the overt sensuality of the place. It is so intensely crowded and chaotic, but at the same time quite surreal and gentle. There seems to be an intense inter-human recognition unlike anything I have ever experienced *en masse*. In the West most public encounters between individuals tend to be meetings of the will. In India I felt that my soul was being caressed by the passing glance of every stranger.

After the first few days I was beginning to feel quite overwhelmed by this new world and by the journey we were about to make. On the fourth day we hired a taxi and made the eight-hour trek to the center of southern India. The countryside there was wild and rustic — sometimes scrubby, sometimes lush — but there was always one consistent feature: people. I don't think a minute passed where there was not a person walking along the side of the road or working in the fields, and yet we were in the middle of nowhere!

We stopped for lunch in a small town (even though it was small, there were thousands of people everywhere). As we alighted from the car, I stretched and looked around the town. In the distance I noticed a man begging with a tin plate. He was surprisingly clean, with long, matted hair and bright saffron robes. There was something austere about him, but as he turned around, I noticed his eyes: They were electrifying. Strong black eyes with a lightning-bolt intensity. I asked Andrew to explain, and he told me that this man was a *Sannyasi,* a man who begs for food as part of his spiritual quest. He continued the explanation over lunch. The magic of India was continuing to intensify.

Several hours later, we pulled up in front of the gates of Saccidananda Ashram. Our arrival had obviously been anticipated, and a crowd came out to greet us. We soon met Father Christudas, a charming little man with a mischievous but delightful smile, and Sister Marie Louise, an old friend and associate of Father Bede, who ran the women's ashram across the road. Father Christudas, we were soon to find out, has been described as Bede's right arm. He ran the ashram (and continues to do so), looking after the administration, work projects, guest accommodations, etc.

Christudas led us to our accommodation, where we dropped off our bags. Mine was a small hut, which, I was soon to realize, I would be sharing with an assortment of creatures. Most of them were inoffensive and posed no danger. I suddenly began to contemplate the daunting task ahead of me. Here I was in the middle of southern India about to make an intimate documentary about a man I had never met. After settling in, Christudas took us to Father Bede.

An incredibly humble man, Bede offered to help in any way he could. He was every bit as charismatic as he had been on that stage in the Sydney auditorium six months before. Over the next four days Andrew and I would spend several hours a day with him. We would audiotape our conversations as we reviewed the questions that we wanted to cover in the film. We were cautious not to delve too deeply, hoping to maintain the spontaneity of our on-screen interviews. During this time I also spoke with ashram residents and staff, scouting for good locations both in the ashram and in surrounding villages.

We had decided to shoot the film over a ten-day period, filming interviews with Father Bede each morning and picking up location footage and other interviews in the afternoons. We were very conscious of Father Bede's age and frailties and organized a schedule that would not be too much of a strain. We also planned to shoot Father Bede going about his daily activities: taking his ritual early morning walk; conducting mass; counseling students; reading and corresponding; and taking meals with ashram guests.

As it turned out, Father Bede would be celebrating his eighty-sixth birthday on the seventh day of our shoot. The ashram and local villagers were planning to make quite a day of this — which provided us an opportunity to get some wonderful footage.

As the shoot progressed, it became clear that we were capturing something very special. Andrew commented that Father Bede's interviews were like direct transmission. Father Christudas mentioned to me one afternoon that Father Bede was "in a state like a candle that has come to the end of its wick and has one last great burst of light before it goes out." This dear old man was sharing every ounce of his experience and knowledge for the benefit of others. His patience and humility were constant. He was prepared to assist in any way he could.

People had come here from all over the world to learn and to heal, and to spend time with this remarkable man. There was something very sacred about his environment. There was a pervasive calm about the place, something that enables one to lay down one's burdens and enjoy the simplicity of this existence. Some afternoons after filming I would take a walk by the river and drink up that feeling of peace: a peace I had seldom felt before or have felt since.

Our return to Sydney saw us with the daunting task of cutting about ten hours of intense interviews down to a television hour. I had no idea how I was going to do this. As I started to watch the material, and as I watched it many times over, the process became clear. The material seemed to have a voice of its own, and so the key elements were more and more obvious.

Before we started the edit, I made a quick trip to London in search of archival material — photographs, film footage, historical documents of Bede's early life — and was blessed in finding some wonderful photos and rare film footage taken during Bede's monastic years.

Our first rough cut of the film ran to just under three hours, or almost three times the commercial running time of a television hour. After several more weeks of reviewing the material, deciding what would have to be cut, and making copious structural changes, we reached a running time of fifty-nine minutes. We were happy that this cut carried Bede's message, with a nice structural balance.

The first public screening in Sydney was very emotional. Father Bede had died only two months prior, and the audience of three hundred were very moved by his appearance on the screen.

The film has now been distributed throughout the world on video and has been broadcast on television in numerous countries. Since the release of *A Human Search* in 1993, we have been overwhelmed with requests for more of our material on Father Bede. We have subsequently released two more videotapes. In addition, many people had requested a written transcription of *A Human Search,* as well as the uncut interviews. And so in late 1995 we decided to publish this book, which includes the content of all the interviews we conducted during the preparation and filming of this documentary. I hope you find this material as rich and inspiring as we have.

— JOHN SWINDELLS

For information on obtaining the 60-minute
VHS video on which this book is based,
please call 1-800-560-MYTH.

1

The Early Years

ALMOST THE ONLY MEMORY I have of my childhood is being with my father in a boat on the Thames. I was about four years old. We were living at Walton-on-Thames near Hampton Court, and I see myself in that boat with my father and there's an atmosphere of joy and of peace. And I think it's significant, now, that it was my father, because he, as I'll explain, had very little place in our lives, but I think he was behind it. Today, after many, many years, I see his place in my life more clearly than I did before. So that memory remains — myself with my father in that boat on the Thames, and that's all.

I was born in Walton-on-Thames, and I lived there for the first four years of my life. Then the event which changed everything took place when my father lost all his money. He was working in a firm — I think it was in the City of London — owned by his uncle. I think that he was a very brilliant person in his way, and his uncle had taken him in as a partner. Then the uncle died, and my father took a partner himself. I think my father was rather inclined to spend freely. The firm was doing well, but after a time the partner said: "Now that you've taken out all your funds, I'll take over." I believe my father brought a lawsuit against the partner. I'm even told he had to go to New York for the trial. But he lost his case, and he never recovered from it, really. He lived in a world of his own; but to us children he was always very kind.

I will say one thing: He was a man without guile. He never said a word against his partner. He looked upon him as a friend. He was rather more antagonistic to my mother's family, but with the partner he never said anything. My father really was a man without guile. But he was still living in a world of his own, totally a world of his own, and he was rather brilliant. I believe he could have stood for Parliament — he was very interested in politics. But things rambled on in his mind and had no relation to actual life — which we regarded as rather a nuisance. He would go on talking and talking all the time. So that was sad, in a way; but now, looking back on it, I feel more and more that he had extraordinary gifts.

One thing stands out very clearly to me now. He sang beautifully — he sang Moody and Sankey's hymns — sitting at the piano. I still recall him sitting at the parents' piano, day after day, singing these hymns. One in particular I recall: "Pull for the shore, sailor, pull for the shore." It must have left an impression on me. Also, I'm recalling now that he used to go off into the countryside visiting churches on his own. He loved the sound of church bells and often used to tell us about the wonderful sound of these bells. He was very Nonconformist. His religion was a hymn-singing religion, and he really enjoyed it; but again, it was all quite apart.

We never spoke about religion. It's a thing we kept apart, each one of us, just as we never spoke about sex. These were two things a person did not discuss in civilized life.

3

There was something very deep behind my father, I think, but as children we missed it. He was so remote from us, really — though he was extremely kind and really loved us, I think, but he couldn't show it, and we couldn't relate to him. That was sad.

Then, on the other side, of course, is my mother. She took charge of the family when my father lost his money. She had a small income. I think some of her family helped her a bit, but we were really very poor — poor middle-class, you would call it. We never actually lacked anything, we had what was really essential, and I'm always grateful for that. It was a basic poverty: We had what was sufficient, but never more than enough. And we got used to making our own bed and preparing the table and washing up and even preparing meals and so on. It was part of our life.

My mother was wonderful. She had been brought up in a rather wealthy middle-class family and was not used to work, yet she really worked day after day to keep the house and keep the family. I think a woman used to come in to help at times, but practically all the work was done with our help. She always provided sufficiently for us. I recall how she would always serve us first, and sometimes there would be hardly anything left for herself. I think she lived a life of totally unselfish love. It comes back to me now, though I didn't realize it at the time, of course, but that's how it really was.

As for her relationship with me — she was very fond of me. I was the fourth child, after two brothers and a sister, arriving after a two- or three-year gap. So I was rather special to my mother, and we had a very special relationship. It was very unconscious on my part, but when I look

4

back on it, it was a relationship of total oneness. We never questioned it or thought about it much, but just took it for granted. Mother was always there. She was the support. She was a firm support, but she didn't really spoil me. Some people thought she did, but she did not. She must have had great control there. She really wanted me to have the best of things and yet not be spoiled in any way.

The most interesting thing in my early childhood was the extraordinary advance in my studies. My mother must have seen that I was rather intelligent in some way and decided that I must be educated. So when I was four, I started French. And by the way, the French master kept an ice-cream shop, and so it was a great attraction to get me to go to the lesson. When I was seven, she got a tutor for me, and I learned Latin. Then I went to a prep school, and at nine I learned Greek. For the next ten years, until I was about nineteen or so, French, Latin, and Greek were my studies.

Of course, this is the background to a very intellectual life. But behind that there was the family life; and we just didn't come into that, really. We did have very normal, natural relationships — when I look back on it, we very rarely quarreled. Although we got on well together, there was very little demonstration of affection or anything like that among us. So it was an extremely peaceful background. You cannot imagine how peaceful the world was before the 1914 war. We hardly ever heard of war or anything like that. There were no disturbances in the neighborhood — no murders or thefts or anything like that. Divorce was practically unknown. When one of our cousins divorced, it was a shock to the whole family. And also, a woman smoking a cigarette was something very rare. We once saw one of my mother's friends — she was a suffragette — smoking, and we were very upset about that. Shocked by it, really. So ours was a very primitive world in a way, but it was very happy. It was extremely happy. When I hear of people today with terrible sufferings, and children being abused, it's amazing to me — our world was like a little paradise, really.

I think it could have been harmful, but it apparently gave me a need for tragedy. So when I learned to read, as I did very early, the more tragic aspects of life attracted me. I read [Sir Walter] Scott's novels when I was ten or eleven, and I loved them. And then I got on to Hardy's *Tess of the d'Urbervilles* and *Jude the Obscure* and Conrad's *Heart of Darkness,* set in the African jungle, then in the Eastern seas and the Pacific and so on. *Lord Jim* was another one of the novels that fascinated me, with all its tragedy and human drama. So human drama and the world of nature were all coming into my life in that way. I would say my life was really lived in these novels and stories.

I lived in those novels far more than in the people I was living with. My whole life was in these wonderful stories: the tragedy and the beauty and the pathos of it all. It was a life lived in the imagination. It occurred to me recently that people in the ancient world lived by myths. In India they lived by the *Mahabharata* and the *Ramayana.* That was their life.

And so for me, it was all this literary life — Hardy in particular. I would recall the return of the native in Dartmoor, which is really Exmoor, where everything is dominated by this moor, this natural landscape. People's lives are molded by the landscape around them. I made a walking tour, later on, of all the Hardy country, and I was fascinated by it.

Then I got on to the Russian novelists — Tolstoy and Dostoevsky. I got through *War and Peace,* and I've never forgotten it. *The Brothers Karamazov,* too, had a tremendous impression on me.

So this was my life. It was really built up with this kind of mythology, if you like. I think that's very interesting. Today, I believe, people are very different. They're brought up in this scientific world with space travel and such things. But I was brought up in more of a romantic world.

And then I got on, of course, to the Romantic poets — Wordsworth, Shelly, and Keats, but especially Wordsworth. He had a very deep influence. I think he said, "I have felt a presence...a sense sublime of something far more deeply interfused, whose dwelling is the light of the setting suns" [from *Tintern Abbey*]. He moves on through nature. I can't remember the words, but he speaks of the sense of a presence in nature working through all creation. That has deeply impressed me.

It all came to a head in an experience I had at the end of school. I had been reading all these things, and I had also got on to the classical writers, as well. Then I walked out one day (I described it in *The Golden String*) by the playing fields in the evening, and I came in touch with a hawthorn bush. It was in flower and it had a very sweet scent, of course. I was overwhelmed by the beauty of it. It was as though I had never smelled or seen anything like it before. And then I went on and stood by a tree, with the sun setting over the playing fields, and a lark rose from my feet and soared aloft, singing and singing, and then sank quietly to rest. The whole scene simply was like a religious ceremony for me. The setting sun seemed to be

7

the scene of the presence of God. And I wasn't particularly religious.

When I was very young, about eight or so, my mother gave me two books to read, *Quiet Talks About Jesus* and *Line Upon Line*. I can't imagine what it would be like now, but obviously at that age something impressed me. Right in the unconscious. At school we didn't refer to it at all, but it was there. This experience sort of made me think of Paradise, and of the angels, and of God. It brought something of the unconscious up to me.

My mother had a very deep spiritual life, but, as I said, we never talked about these things. From the age of four or five, I think, I used to say my prayers every evening — "God bless Father and Mother and bless my family." Also, we always went to the village church (my mother had her very simple Anglican religion). It was just part of our world and just simply spontaneous and natural. And we rather enjoyed the singing and the parson — a very attractive person who gave very short sermons.

My mother had her own personal piety. I will always recall, when I would come to say goodnight to her, very often she would be leaning by the bed in prayer. That left a deep impression on me. Obviously her life was sustained by prayer, far more than I imagined at the time.

So I grew up with a background of religion, but it was very much in the background, because we didn't talk about it and we really didn't think about it much. But there's no doubt it did sustain our life. Both my father and my mother contributed a religious background to my life.

Then, toward the end of her lifetime, my mother told me a story. She must have been very exhausted at times. And

8

she told me that she was almost at the end of her strength once, and she looked in the mirror and saw herself there and a strange light was around her. I've never doubted this at all. A simple woman, who gives her life for her family, and works day by day and does not talk about it — she's very close to God. I think it was a sign of blessing on her life, really.

Of course, I feel I owe everything to that. To have a family background like that, and that amount of order in your life, is a tremendous power. We see many people whose lives are so full of tragedy because they don't have the mother's love. I realize more and more what a grace it was for me. I keep looking back on that and feel that the mother — and it's not only my mother, but "the Mother" — is behind me all the time.

So when I reflect now as a Catholic, the Virgin Mary has this place of the Mother. And particularly, I think of the Black Madonna — the mother of the earth and the whole creation, the mother who is in the life of the plants, the animals, the whole world, and all human life. So for me, "mother" means Mother Nature, Mother Earth, mother of the living world and the human world, and my own mother. They all come together in the Virgin Mother, and it's very, very deep now. As I look back, I begin to see more and more how these things have grown. It was something very important in my life.

I think I was a very ordinary child, though I must mention one thing that I recalled recently. Apparently, some told me, when I was very young, I had a companion named Harold, and whenever anything unfortunate happened I always referred it to Harold. He was the cause of it all. I don't remember any of this, of course, but my sister and others told me about it. So maybe I was a little odd in that way, but otherwise I was a very normal child and enjoyed playing all the normal games. It was an open-air life. Children just ran about freely, and I was always on the bicycle. I loved bicycling all around, and even racing. There was a very natural background to our life.

I also had a very great attraction to music. I began to learn the piano at a pretty early age, and I kept it up for ten or twelve years. When I was at school, I had a teacher who helped me a good deal, and so I practiced regularly. I read music very slowly, but once I learned it, I knew it by heart. I had quite a repertoire: Schumann, Schubert, Chopin, and Beethoven sonatas. Toward the end I went on to Bach — the Preludes and the Fugues.

So there was a real evolution in my musical interest and ability. I must have been pretty good — probably the best boy in the school — because I was chosen to play at the school concert. I played Debussy's "Clair de Lune." I still remember it. One man I know said afterward that it was worth coming all the distance he had come just to listen to that one thing. So it must have given him something. I loved playing. Whenever I went visiting, people always asked me to play, and I was glad I had this repertoire. So music was quite a big thing in my young life. When I went to Oxford, though, I dropped it all, and I've never played since.

My first ambition was to be a driver of a steamroller. I had seen one outside our house, mending the road, and I saw a man sitting on this huge machine, sort of dominating the world. And I thought, *Now that's what I want to be.* So that was my first dream. And then we knew someone in the navy. He was a midshipman, and he was a great friend. He was a role model for all our games, and so I decided to go into the navy. I don't think he really encouraged me, but I certainly thought that my plan would be to become an admiral of the fleet. I always seemed to want to get to the top. It was extraordinary. So that was my second dream . . . until I went to public school. Then, I remember, an older boy there spoke to me and said, "You're not made for mathematics and such. You're made for the classics. No good your going in the navy." So I switched around and decided to join the Indian civil service, which was quite a big thing at that time. It turned out, though, when I left Oxford, most of the Indians had taken over the civil service, so I wasn't needed. My ambition at that time was to become viceroy of India. That was quite clear in my mind. I don't think that the ICS normally leads to that, but I thought it might be the way. Obviously, I had some tremendous ambition to be at the top all the time — probably very bad, but there it was.

I went to a preparatory school called Furzie Close, at Barton-on-Sea, when I was about eight. As my family were very poor, I was allowed to go as a day boy. I was the only day boy there. All the others were boarders and paid higher fees. That marked me out to some extent, but I enjoyed the life. The lessons were very good and, incidentally, I might say that I rewarded the school, because in the end I passed first in all England in a public examination for Christ's Hospital. So they were pleased in the end.

Furzie Close was a typical private school of that time, run by a man and his wife who were simply little lord and lady there. They managed the whole thing on their own. They were good people in their way, but both of them were very dominating, and there was an atmosphere of fear in the place. Sometimes it was quite shocking the way they treated a boy if they felt he behaved badly. They would publicly abuse him. This fear remained all through my school days. We were always afraid of the masters.

On the other hand, we were very healthy and happy boys. I must tell another incident, which was very bad. In 1914, there was a clergyman who came to teach in the school, and these wretched boys thought that he ought to join up and they would shout at him: "John, John, get your khaki on." They did that sort of thing — little boys can be demons. All these things went on, but it was an extremely happy life there. Of course, I did very well at school, both in games and also in my studies.

I started at Christ's Hospital when I was about twelve years old. The school had been founded by Edward VI. My having excelled in the exam for admission delighted my mother very much. I recall an incident in the train when she was talking to another woman, who said proudly, "My son also is going to Christ's Hospital, and he passed second." And my mother said, "Ah, my son passed first," making quite a thing of it. When I arrived, I was put right on to a higher grade — actually the middle form — having skipped the lower forms altogether.

So I would say I probably reached the pinnacle of my intellectual ratings when I was about twelve. After that I began to decline.

Christ's Hospital was a good experience, but like the previous place, there was fear. The masters were very strict: You learned all the Latin and Greek grammar and all that, and if you made a single mistake, you were put down for it. And you were beaten if you made too many mistakes. It took us about two or three years to get beyond this fear. But it was a good education without a doubt. The headmaster, Dr. Upcott, was a doctor of divinity. He wore a magnificent red robe, and I never forgot his giving us a talk about the "religious, royal and ancient foundations of Christ Hospital. May God bless those who bless those who love it..." or something like that.

When we got on to the sixth and top form, called Grecians, we were allowed a great deal of liberty, and we all wore this Tudor uniform with knee breeches, orange stockings, and a blue coat which had silver buttons with Edward VI's figure on them. It was the most magnificent thing, with velvet cuffs and a velvet collar, big buttons going right down, and a broad girdle. So a Grecian was a very important person.

In fact, I remember somebody saying that I went about the school as though I owned the place. It was very good experience, because we Grecians had a great deal of liberty.

When I got on to the sixth form, the headmaster was W. H. Fyfe. He succeeded Dr. Upcott. He was the first headmaster to be a layman. He was a fellow of Merton College at Oxford, but a great humanist. This was my first encounter with humanism, and he opened up the library to the boys. It was an excellent library. I was fascinated with the complete set of the works of Shakespeare. There were also complete sets of Hardy and Conrad, Jane Austen, and all these writers who had been my life for years. In our classical studies, by that time, we could read Plato and Homer in Greek fairly easily, and we were encouraged to get texts on our own to read for ourselves. So we really went deeply into it. It was a very good education and one that occupied me for a long time.

In this library there was everything that I loved. The sixth-form boys used to meet in the headmaster's house on a Sunday and share together. I read a paper there once on the year 1880 as being the great time of the aesthetic revival. Fyfe was a very wonderful person and became a very good friend to me. I always recall the time we were doing a Greek Testament lesson with him, and when we came onto the subject of the Virgin Birth, we all challenged him: "Now, do you believe in the Virgin Birth?" And he said, "What does it matter?" That was his view. He was a real Christian humanist. And he preached sermons in the school chapel — not from the pulpit, which was a long way away, but from the lectern in the middle. And he enchanted. We didn't listen to the sermons there normally, but we listened to every word he said. So after he left, he became a very good friend and remained so until the end of his life.

There was another incident that was quite interesting. We became pacifists toward the end of school, after reading Tolstoy's *Kingdom of Heaven*. We were all supposed to join the Officers Training Corps (OTC), and word went around that we were to be made corporals in this, that we were going to go up in rank. Three of us who felt very strongly on the subject decided we were not going to take rank (one of them ended up as foreign minister in a Labour government, incidentally). So we went to the head of the Corps, who was a very interesting man, actually, and told him we didn't approve of this. And he said, "You had better. I'm old enough to be your father. You should be guided by me..."

and so on. And we replied, "Tolstoy's old enough to be your father, and you should listen to Tolstoy." So we were very rebellious; but the headmaster took it beautifully, as he always did.

Incidentally, the head of the Corps once said that the headmaster's work in a school was a combination of a telephone exchange and an oilcan. You had to keep people in touch, and then you had to oil the works when it didn't work properly. He was wonderful like that. And so he let us off the Corps altogether.

So I didn't have the Corps and I didn't have games, and I was free to go into the Sussex country, ride my bicycle along the countryside, and stop to read poetry. That was my life then. Nature and poetry were my whole life. We went to the chapel every morning and twice on Sundays, and I enjoyed the singing and the atmosphere. I must say there was a beautiful mural in the chapel. Frank Branigan did paintings of the apostles all around the chapel, and I was facing a wonderful painting of Saint Stephen being martyred, wearing a gorgeous orange robe. I have never forgotten it. So that was something to enliven one's life. We took the school chapel as something that we enjoyed — particularly the singing. But otherwise, the religious life was almost nil.

Toward the end of the time before I was supposed to be confirmed, I had to do the catechism with my housemaster. He had no interest in it at all, and I had no interest in it at all, so it was a purely mechanical process. Which was very sad, because it could have been a moment of opening up the spiritual life, but it meant absolutely nil at that point. So when I went up to Oxford, I had no religion of any sort, really, except the love of nature and of poetry. They were the whole heart of my religion.

During this period of school, when I was, I suppose, about seventeen, my life centered on reading novels and poetry, particularly the Romantic poets, and above all Wordsworth, who still remains for me a very profound influence because of his cosmic religion. He found God in nature. That was really what I was seeking. I loved to quote the lines written about Tintern Abbey. Tintern Abbey, of course, recalls the whole past history of England and Cistercian monks and so on. This is what Wordsworth wrote:

> For I have learned
> To look on nature, not as in the hour
> Of thoughtless youth; but hearing oftentimes,
> The still, sad music of humanity,
> Nor harsh nor grating, though of ample power
> To chasten and subdue. And I have felt
> A presence that disturbs me with the joy
> Of elevated thoughts; a sense sublime
> Of something far more deeply interfused
> Whose dwelling is the light of setting suns,
> And the round ocean and the living air,
> And the blue sky, and in the mind of man:
> A motion and a spirit, that impels
> All thinking things, all objects of all thought,
> And rolls through all things.

You can call that pantheism if you like, but really it's the awareness of the presence of God in nature. And that remained with me, and remains with me today, as absolutely fundamental in my life. I always cherish it. But

I also remember now some lines from the *Ode: Intimations of Immortality from Recollections of Early Childhood.* Wordsworth says:

> Not in entire forgetfulness,
> And not in utter nakedness,
> But trailing clouds of glory do we come
> From God, who is our home:
> Heaven lies about us in our infancy!

Then he goes on:

> Shades of the prison-house begin to close
> Upon the growing Boy,

I think this is the history of humanity. We all come out of a golden age, the paradise. All ancient people have a knowledge of an age when all was bliss and peace reigned. And then we come into this prison house. But of course we must not exaggerate. It's a golden age of childhood, but we have to grow. We have to eat of the Tree of Knowledge of Good and Evil. It brings us down, but it gives us a knowledge that we could not otherwise have. We have to go beyond and return to the source.

That's our calling today. We have fallen away from the golden age, the paradise. We are living in this world of conflict and this prison house, but we are being called back all the time to the transcendent mystery. To return to paradise. That's the goal of humanity, really.

So Wordsworth is still a very vital force, I think, and his cosmic religion is what we need today — the presence of God in the whole of creation. Most people have lost that, and we need to recover it.

More and more, I began to ride out to the Sussex country-side. I still remember little vivid images of seeing some wild roses growing by the roadside and the sort of ecstasy it produced while riding on my bicycle. I can also remember the scent of some lime blossoms. Little recollections like that come back. They must have imprinted themselves deep in my psyche. They simply come back now, memories from the Sussex countryside.

On Sundays we used to go out and get apples from the local farms; we enjoyed that immensely. When I left school and went to Oxford, we were living near Newbury and Reading, in a house on a common there. I used to go and watch all the local birds and look at the flowers. I got to know all of them. I used to take long walks in the woods and in the hills. Every day, I think it was after lunch, I used to walk out for several hours and spend time with nature like that. And behind it all was always this original experience of it — a kind of ecstasy and the feeling that I wanted to return to nature, recover that experience which I had had. Of course, you can never do this. I remember C. S. Lewis telling me: "You always want to recover that paradisal experience, but you cannot. You have to go forward through the struggle, the pain, to something beyond."

But that desire still remained with me for all those years that we were living in Newbury.

2

The Shaping of the Mind – College Days

THE ARRIVAL at Oxford in October 1925 was, of course, a great event. Here you were no longer a schoolboy; you became a gentleman. This gave you a great sense of status at the time. It opened up a whole new world. People addressed me as Mr. Griffiths. And I was very taken with the beauty of Oxford, the High Street, and above all, of Magdalen College, where I was enrolled. I chose Magdalen because I thought it was the most beautiful college at Oxford. It answered all my needs and prayers. I had a room in the first year overlooking the deer park. The next year my room looked over the Magdalen Tower and the cloisters with the river walks in the background. By day we would go out along the river walks, and then we would take a punt or a canoe on the river. Most of my reading in English literature was done on the river. So it was a wonderful setting in that way.

But Magdalen had a shadow side. It is very much a resort of old Etonians. I always recall what Chesterton said: "Oxford is the playground of the idle rich." There were many people in Magdalen just like that. They used to get drunk and run around the cloisters shouting and singing and so on — which I suppose was quite normal. But there

20

was the other side: For the scholars like myself who had to live rather cheaply and work very hard, they gave you every encouragement to study. (I later found out that C. S. Lewis joined Magdalen as a tutor the same term that I joined as an undergraduate.) The atmosphere at that time, after the First World War, was an atmosphere of disenchantment. (C. Montague wrote a book called *Disenchantment*, which caught that atmosphere extremely well.) There was a sense of disillusionment, that life had no real meaning. All my friends who studied philosophy said, "You cannot learn any truth from philosophy, and so you try to enjoy yourself. You go to the cinema, drink beer, and have a good time." But there was a search behind that, all the time. For my friends and me, the search was for meaning.

I had this great friend, Frank Root. He went up to Oxford before me and showed me around when I got there. He was an ardent pacifist and member of the Labour party, and he was in our group at school when we had protested against taking rank in the OTC. Besides Root and myself, there was also Michael Stuart (another strong leader of the Labour party, who later became a foreign minister). It was the three of us who had gone to the head of the Corps to protest: "We are not going to take our rank in the Corps. We don't agree with war at all," whereupon he lectured us on the rights of war and our duty to our country. The headmaster was wonderful about this. He let us off the Corps altogether.

The first thing I did with my friend Root at Oxford was join the "No More War" Movement. We used to go to all the meetings. He introduced me to the Union at Oxford where all the best speakers came. The Labour party was getting very strong, and Michael Stuart became one of the leaders of the Peace Union while I was there. The movement was leaning toward Socialism then, and Ramsay MacDonald was prime minister. We were devoted to him.

So much for the political background. Suffice it to say it prepared us for what was to come. We saw the shift from Socialism to Communism, and then the reaction of Fascism and Hitler in the 1930s.

In 1926 there was a general strike in England, and I took the miners' side. My friends and I had studied the case carefully and were convinced that they were right, which did not make us popular in Oxford. But I still feel it was a worthwhile stand to take. I even ended up offering to sell the *Daily Worker* in the streets.

By that time I was disillusioned with all of civilization, not just what I saw and lived through. I think T. S. Eliot's *Wasteland* and *The Hollow Men* brought out the sense that civilization was collapsing. That made us turn to poetry, to art, to music, to another world altogether. For me, it became a friendship with Hugh Waterman and Martyn Skinner, my two greatest friends at Oxford. We have continued our friendship right up to the present time. Hugh died two or three years ago, but Martyn is still alive, and we still correspond. We were all in reaction against the whole industrial civilization. Martyn was a poet. He wrote heroic couplets in the style of prose, denouncing people and so on. When he met Hugh, who was a much more poetic and sympathetic character altogether, he became very much more gentle. We felt that nature and poetry were our religion, really; it was a religion of beauty.

When I met Hugh, we were sitting at a table in Magdalen. Without any introduction, he turned to me and said, "Do you like the letters of Keats?" It was an extraordinary remark in a way, but it just struck exactly the right note for me, because Keats stood for this philosophy of beauty. I always remember Keats' words: "I am certain of nothing but the holiness of the heart's affections, and the truth of Imagination," and that was our religion. The truth of the imagination, not of science and rational thinking, but of intuitive poetic thinking. That led to a whole aesthetic religion, really.

At that time Oxford was divided between the aesthetes and the athletes. The athletes played games and went hunting and enjoyed themselves. We were aesthetes. Our two patron saints were Walter Pater and Oscar Wilde. We were quite serious. Ours was a real search for beauty in life; it was not fantasy. Beauty in daily life, and beauty in the whole of nature. So it really became a religion for us, this religion of beauty — going all the way back to Plato — then opening onto the Romantic poets and so on.

A turning pointing came in my third year, when I gave up classics, or more specifically I completed the classics course. I find it interesting that the one really good paper I wrote was on Greek sculpture. I was deeply impressed with this. But then I took up English literature, and that led me to meet C. S. Lewis. He became my tutor. It was very interesting that he was just coming out of his romantic phase. He wrote a poem called "Dymer" under the name of Clive Hamilton. It was a very romantic poem, but he was coming out of that toward a more balanced philosophy. He wasn't a Christian at all at the time, of course, any more than I was. And so we met, really, on this level of romanticism

23

and philosophy. If I remember correctly, his first book was *The Great Divorce.** This was in favor of reason and romanticism. He was trying to blend, as I was also actually gradually learning to do, the romantic sense of beauty of nature and love with the reason of the more austere kind of intellectual development.

So these were my influences — Root with the socialism and pacifism and Martyn with his poetry. And I should say that Martyn became a serious poet. He received the Hawthornden Prize in 1943 for his *Letters to Malaya,* which was on the subject of the War. Then he wrote a long poem called *The Return of Arthur,* in Chaucerian standards, which has never really received proper acclaim. It's a miraculous work of art. He really had a mastery of words and rhyme. His work is fantastic, but it's also serious. I think there are lines of profound beauty, where he showed a deep love for nature. He would go out at night and spend hours under the moonlight, simply living in the life of nature. He also wrote heroic couplets at school, in the manner of Pope, a very cynical style. But under the influence of Hugh, who was much more of a humanist, I would say he became more concerned with the whole Romantic Movement and the love of nature.

So there was something very deep in Martyn. Hugh and I shared this Keatsian vision of beauty as the truth of the imagination. We thought you find truth not merely through abstract philosophical thought and scientific study but through intuitive awareness of nature and of love. Keats

---

*Lewis's first book was actually *The Pilgrim's Regress* (1933). *The Great Divorce* was published in 1945, after Lewis had already published five novels and sundry works of theology and literary criticism.

expressed this exactly for us. In his "Ode on a Grecian Urn," he says " 'Beauty is truth, truth beauty,' — that is all / Ye know on earth, and all ye need to know." And that's what we felt.

We tried to live according to this religion of beauty, and it brought us up against the Industrial Revolution. Martyn felt it more than any of us, but we all felt it. It was destroying the beauty of the world and, I would say, the sacredness of the world, and we felt that very strongly. So we tried to get away from Oxford at every opportunity. Martyn had a car, and we would just go out. Of course, we took the Industrial Revolution with us, but still we got out and went to Tintern Abbey and saw all the beautiful sights in England.

Perhaps the most important break was when we left Oxford on a motor tour of Cambridge, which is much more peaceful than Oxford. Modern technology moved in on Oxford, and that really upset things.* Cambridge is so much more of a university town, and we were impressed with the beauty there. We went to Ely Cathedral there and to Peterborough and then to Lincoln Cathedral and to York Minster — all those medieval sites. The architecture absolutely captivated us, not from a religious but from an aesthetic point of view. I particularly remember Peterborough. It was a very industrialized city and a dirty place, and it had this cathedral rising up like a dream from another world. It opened up the whole other world to us. At the end of the trip we went around to the Lake District, where Wordsworth had lived, and we stayed at Ullswater.

---

*New housing estates in the new town of Cowley, and especially car-manufacturing factories, upset the rather non-industrial academic old town of Oxford — causing a great tension between "town" and "gown."

All that world of nature that Wordsworth had discovered came back to us. I recall that I went up into the hills and was completely alone, and a mist came over and I felt as if I was alone in the universe — a sort of total emptiness, and yet total bliss, was there. It was a wonderful experience.

So, it seemed as if things were going now from the political to the aesthetic. And the aesthetic appreciation was steadily leading us to a religious phase. It was not formal religion in any sense, and perhaps this is important, because millions of people today are outgrowing the whole industrial system and are searching for a deeper meaning. Art and poetry, beauty and sensitivity: These lead us out of the system. For us, then, it was an important stage in our lives.

When I first went up to Oxford, I was definitely one of the aesthetes. I had a romantic love of clothes. I remember looking in the shop windows at a green or purple shirt and wondering when I would have enough money to buy it. That was part of this mood of discontent: [this desire] for beauty in one's life, thinking that beauty was central to the meaning of life — or that it gave life meaning. My room in Oxford was on the second floor. It was beautiful, with white paneling, and I had hung two beautiful Japanese color prints. I had gone to the British Museum, where I met Lawrence Binyon, a guide who showed me Japanese prints. In fact, he actually selected them for me. It was very interesting having such a guide. Also, I had a William Morris tapestry, which I hung on the door. I was surrounded with that kind of atmosphere. I also had a statue of the Aphrodite of Mylos always in front of me. This was my world at that time. Beauty was the meaning of it all.

I didn't play the piano anymore after I went up to Oxford, but we were all deeply in love with music. Hugh and Martyn had all the last quartets of Beethoven, and these enchanted us. They came at the end of his life when he seemed to have passed beyond all normal human feeling, and on to a transcendent mystery. It was very mystical music, I think, and again, it sort of foretold the future. It was pushing me into a more mystical understanding.

Hugh also had a copy of Botticelli's "Primavera."

In a sense, for us this was an awakening to the whole world; and in a curious way I still live back in that time. My memories come back, and I live the life I did when I was eighteen or nineteen — still today. It's fascinating. Music was very important in our lives and was the one thing that most of the undergraduates took seriously. They went to all the concerts. We had these beautiful string quartets and polyphonic music that enchanted us. It had a serious and lasting influence.

All these things came together: the beauty of nature and art, with politics in the background. It was a coming, I suppose, to maturity. I think you live out only what you experience — and then through the rest of your life. In a way, you bring out what was implicit from the beginning.

Another very important influence on me at this time was a friend, Hugh L'Anson Fausset, who lived near us in Newbury. He was himself a very good writer. He wrote very critical books on Coleridge and Tolstoy, and he studied the Romantic Movement much more thoroughly than I had. And he understood it much more deeply. He introduced me to the works of D. H. Lawrence and the whole world of the dawning unconscious, which later Carl Jung explored more fully. I was impressed by Lawrence's *Fantasia of the Uncon-*

scious, and then his *Women in Love.* I've been rereading it lately, and I found a passage that expertly expresses what I believe today. I think D. H Lawrence through his sex experience came to genuine mystical experience of transcendent reality. There seemed to be no doubt. He writes:

> In the new, superfine bliss, a peace superseding knowledge, there was no I and you, there was only the third, unrealized wonder, the wonder of existing not as oneself, but in a consummation of my being and of her being in a new, paradisal unit regained from the duality. How can I say "I love you" when I have ceased to be, and you have ceased to be: we are both caught up and transcended into a new oneness where everything is silent, because there is nothing to answer, all is perfect and at one. Speech travels between the separate parts. But in the perfect One there is perfect silence of bliss.

That's what *saccidananda* means — the fullness of bliss in life. So, Lawrence had a very deep experience, and he brought together all this love of nature.

Of course, the question of sex came up all the time at Oxford, and many felt you should just enjoy yourself, but I think we learned the sacredness of sex. I think this is very important: It's the only answer, actually. It does no good treating sex as simply natural, and it's still worse if you treat it as unnatural. It has to be consecrated. It's holy and it has to be consecrated. Then it comes from one of the most powerful forces in human nature. The great mystics like Saint John of the Cross all transformed sex. In their writings they use love imagery all the time. People say, "Oh, no, it's nothing to do with that. It's purely spiritual." That's nonsense. The Spirit is taking possession of the body, its senses and feelings, and transfiguring it all. That's what we were trying to learn at Oxford. Not to leave the body nor to simply indulge it, but to undergo it. Undergo! It has to happen. We must undergo the transformation. I owe everything I learned about this to D. H. Lawrence.

A turning point came at the end of my second year after I took the "Honour Mods," as it is called, in Latin and Greek. I decided I'd had enough of all this intellectual stuff. I wanted more poetry and beauty in my life, so I decided to read English literature. That meant that I had C. S. Lewis as my tutor. We met in 1928, and we became great friends. Actually, the friendship lasted for many years. I remember when I last saw him, he said, "Do you realize that we've been friends for forty years?"

At Oxford, we had to write a paper every week. The one thing you had to do, if you didn't do anything else, was produce a paper every week. That meant that you sat with your tutor and he criticized it. Lewis had the most wonderful, accurate, and perceptive mind. They say, and I believe it's true, he could quote from almost any poet in English if you simply opened the quotation. If somebody read out a line of poetry, he'd say, "Yes, I've got it" and simply continue the poem. It was a real education to be with him. Our conversations went on and on. I'd meet with him about eight o'clock in the evening and sometimes we'd go on to midnight, exchanging views on everything.

We had only two quarrels that I remember. I wrote an article on Milton. I can't remember exactly what position I took, but for some reason — I'm not sure why — he took offense to it very much, and he put me down very severely.

29

But it passed over. Otherwise we had a wonderful relationship with each other. When I first met him, I told Lewis about why I had left the classics and was coming to English literature — to develop the beauty of the imagination and emotions and so on — and he was most indignant. He was just then getting out of that himself and wanted a much more classical intellectual approach. We had quite an argument over that. He was in protest against the whole aesthetic movement.

Of course, he was a big influence on my becoming a Christian. We were almost contemporary with that. We began to discover the Christian background of English literature. I remember in particular William Law's *Spirit of Love* and *Spirit of Prayer* and Bishop Butler's *Analogy of Religion*. Reading had a big effect on us; we were approaching it from a philosophical point of view. (I must mention that Lewis put me on to reading philosophy and Berkeley's *Principles of Human Knowledge.*)

C. S. Lewis looked like a North Ireland farmer, with a sort of florid countenance, and was rather fat. He drank beer and smoked a pipe. He dressed in rather rough tweed things, and he went out with a dog. You could say he was really a sort of deliberate rejection of the whole aesthetic movement. We were total opposites at that time. It's so often the way that opposites really enrich each other. That's how we grew. I owe a tremendous amount to his influence in my becoming a Christian — actually, I believe it was mutual. We shared with each other.

I think it's significant that Lewis went back to being a Protestant. (He was Northern Irish, of course.) But I always felt his Christianity was too limited. For instance, and this

30

is a very simple thing: He never accepted criticism of the New Testament. He had an almost naive view of the way the gospels are composed. I felt that was a real limitation. I thought that in becoming a Catholic I'd have become much more narrow, but actually it led me on the way to a much broader interpretation. So I feel less near to Lewis now than I did in the early years.

When I left Oxford, C. S. Lewis advised me to read philosophy. Normally, I would have gone on from the Honour Mods to study the Greeks and read the philosophy of Plato and Aristotle. But I had switched across to English literature, and he thought I ought to go back to philosophy. So I began to read quite seriously. One of the first was Spinoza, which had a very deep effect on me. You see, I think I was getting away from my romanticism and I wanted a dose of pure reason. Spinoza, as I found later in the writings of Saint Thomas Aquinas, had an almost geometric style and exact rational knowledge. For the first time I began to criticize my experience of God, and beauty, and love, and to give it a rational basis. What impressed me more than anything was Spinoza's intellectual love. You join your intellect with love. I found it later again in Dante. This to me was the key.

At this time we were all rebelling against an abstract inhuman rationalism. What I think I learned from Spinoza is that you could use all these and to their fullest extent and then introduce love at the very heart of it; that was something new.

I then read Descartes. What impressed me was starting all over again to get a rational view of the universe. I didn't know the defects of Descartes at that time.

Then I went on to read Berkeley; his *Principles of Human Knowledge* gave me the understanding that there was a mind behind the universe. This was a tremendous breakthrough. Particularly the passage where he says: "Some truths there are so near and obvious to the mind that man need only open his mind to perceive them.... "

Some have gone on studying the universe while totally ignoring their mind. They've never observed their mind. Today, this is where the breakthrough is taking place. People are beginning to see that they cannot study the universe unless they also study human consciousness; it's a meeting of the two.

Which brings us to the point that Plato discovered. Aristotle describes how the early Greek philosophers said that the meaning of the universe is in the water or the air or the fire. And then Socrates came and said, *No, the origin is in the mind.* And that's breakthrough: when you begin to see that the water and the air and the fire are all governed, controlled, by a mind.

Today, I think, we are recovering this. We don't have to have the quite pure idealism of Berkeley, but we do realize that we only know the universe when the human mind meets with the energy that pervades the universe; and then we discover the reality of the universe is the meeting of the human mind with this energy that pervades everything. So Berkeley still remains for me a guide. And the fact that he was a bishop in the Church of Ireland meant a lot to me. You see, I never thought that Christians could think properly like that, at that time. Mind you, the kind of Christianity we were presented with did not offer any serious thought, really. So it was a natural illusion, in a way. But for me, that was one

32

of the stepping-stones toward seeing that Christianity had a rational basis to it.

The *Confessions of Saint Augustine* was another kind of landmark work. Here was a great Christian saint, and even a Catholic, giving me a vision of reality that was profoundly philosophical and yet also profoundly moving. It was love in the search for truth, and that was what I was looking for. It also included beauty. Saint Augustine was a Neoplatonist, and Plato had seen beauty as the ideal of all. Augustine wrote, "O Beauty so ancient and so new, too late have I loved thee...." And that's exactly what we were looking for. Beauty transcending all, which engaged your love totally. And then Augustine brings to it an incredibly deep intelligence. Reading the last chapters of the *Confessions,* where he interprets the Bible with a profound symbolic mystical understanding, taught me something totally new. I was used to Samuel Butler and Bernard Shaw interpreting the Bible, and, of course, they can make nonsense of it very easily. But Augustine was a real breakthrough for me — especially seeing this great mind interpret the Bible in the deep mystical, symbolic sense, putting me on the track of real wisdom, real understanding.

Dante's *Divine Comedy* was a further stage in my enlightenment, if you like to call it that. It was not so much the *Paradiso,* which really was beyond me; it was the *Purgatorio* — the experience you have to go through, the purification of your passions, of your emotions. This was different from Shelley and the others who advocated that you should simply let your emotions flow. That can be very beautiful for a time, but the emotions are always ambivalent, so they lead you into disaster. Dante taught me how the emotions and the passions can be brought under an inner guidance of your mind and will and open up to God, to the transcendent. And, of course, Dante's relation to Beatrice is beautiful. He falls in love with this girl. It's a perfect, total love, but he doesn't go and indulge it. He keeps it within and allows it to grow, and it becomes a pure spiritual love. She takes him to paradise in the end. It's a wonderful parable of how love can be transformed. That's what I was learning, and I think that's what we all have to learn. Many find it very difficult.

Many feel sex is a wonderful thing and a marvelous experience. But if you simply go into it, it has a terrible negative side, and it can destroy you in the end. And if you simply reject it, then you reject part of your whole human nature. We must learn how to love the sex energy, the love energy: to open up, to grow, to mature, to be informed by intelligence and by a human will, and opened up to the transcendent.

I discovered Aquinas through C. S. Lewis's friend Owen Barfield, who was reading Aquinas at the time. He had been studying Dante before going on to Aquinas. It was the first time that I'd ever thought of Aquinas. So I went on to read his *Summa Theologica* in Latin. It was very much like Spinoza, with the same exact lucid, rational thinking and yet informed by not only extreme intelligence, but also profound love. Aquinas was a mystic, and he apparently read Dionysius the Areopagite when he was twenty-seven years old. He wrote a commentary on it.

Behind all this rational theology there is a profound mystical awareness. After we'd gone through Augustine and Dante, Aquinas gave a sort of final theological statement. At that point I really got beyond the limits of philosophy, and I began to discover the theological tradition. The whole Catholic Church then opened up to me. It was very surprising, and it took time for me to absorb it all. Aquinas gave the most rational understanding I could have of the whole biblical and Christian tradition. At the same time his mind was informed by a deep mystical awareness. He did not leave you in the desert of rational thought but opened you up to the mystery of love in the end.

So much that Aquinas says about love is so meaningful — the whole idea that love is union, that when two people love each other, they give themselves to each other. You lose yourself in the other. The other loses themselves [sic] in you, and you find another that is neither you nor they. This is exactly what D. H. Lawrence had found. And that's why I can honestly say that D. H. Lawrence took me right into Saint Thomas Aquinas. And that's where I reached the goal.

3

Eastington – An Experiment in Communal Life

WHEN WE LEFT OXFORD, we had no idea what life was really about. We were confused. Our philosophy studies didn't seem to prepare us to go anywhere. We did have a great love and devotion for nature and poetry, but we had no place in the world.

The year was 1929, and there seemed to be great confusion everywhere. Those once interested in the Socialist Movement were moving toward Communism. One of my greatest friends at Oxford told me he had ceased to be a "pink Socialist" and had become a "red Communist." Along with such a change came opposition to Fascism and Nazism. This period was a very crucial moment in European history. We felt called to go out of the whole political system — whether communist, capitalist, or whatever — to get beyond the confusion. In short, we tried to escape. We went to the west coast of Ireland and other remote, rural places like that, to get away from the confusion of urban civilized life. We felt that we didn't belong in the city, in a system that was destroying the world's beauty. We wanted to belong to the countryside. I ventured to a village in the Cotswolds with my two friends, Hugh and Martyn. They both had money. Martyn's father was an extremely wealthy man and stood for all that we objected to in the industrial system. But since Martyn and Hugh provided the money, I was taken in. We got a little four-room cottage in the village of Eastington, near Northleach. It was a tiny little village of just two hundred or three hundred people — very simple people. But it was very beautiful. Each house was built of stone and had a stone-tiled roof, a pigsty, and a little garden. It was not self-supporting, but there was a basic self-support there.

Here we could be in touch with beauty, with sacredness. We wanted nothing to do with the profane world that was dominating at the time, coming into Oxford and spreading everywhere. We wanted to get free of all that and go back to a basic, simple life.

So we managed to acquire this cottage. It cost five hundred pounds at that time. It was now 1939, and we reckoned that the standard of living being as it was in the village, the three of us would be able to live in that cottage — with all necessities of life (including books) — on a hundred pounds a year. We would spend that amount in a few days back home. So we were really living a radically simple life.

Next door to us was another small cottage where there lived a young man and his wife. He was driving a lorry at the time, but his family were all farmers. So he gave up his lorry and settled in the village with us and bought some cows and taught us to milk them. Every morning at six o'clock we would be out at sunrise, going to the cowshed and milking the cows. This was a sort of primitive simplicity, but it was wonderful. Our neighbor was a great help to us in every way. He was a very practical man. He told us his father was a shepherd and had been in this village for his whole life, and that he had brought up the family of five on twelve shillings and sixpence a week. It's almost unbelievable! But they had all they wanted.

We really aspired to live in this very primitive, simple style and were very anxious to have the utmost simplicity in our furniture. So we got some wheel-back chairs and a table. They were very simple, very beautiful, too. And we put coconut matting on the floor. Then we had a problem with crockery. There was a van that used to come into the village from a neighboring town, selling modern crockery, which we thought we would have to get. But then to our delight we found there was a potter in the neighborhood — Michael Cardew — who was doing beautiful English slipware. He was prepared to provide us with everything we needed. We even had a beautiful water pot. We had to go to the village tap to get water. I believe in earlier years you had to go to the spring, which was quite a distance away. When it was freezing outside, though, you had to light a fire to melt the ice first. Then you put your water in these beautiful vessels. Going out at dawn to get water was a wonderful experience.

We had a beautiful routine in our kitchen. In the morning we prepared vegetables and meat — we would get meat at that time — and put it all in a pot and boil it up. Then we would put the pot in a hay box and let it simmer for the rest of the morning. By the time we washed at midday, it was ready to eat — and it was very juicy and very good. We also had four Khaki-Campbell ducks, and they laid four eggs every day. There were only three of us, and only occasionally did we have guests, so the food provided all that we needed. For bread we went to a mill in the neighboring town, Northleach, where they made a stone-ground flour. It's very interesting that in previous years almost all the grain was ground in these stone mills by the river. Now all the water power went to Cirencester to power machinery, but we were still in touch with an earlier simplicity.

We also wanted cheese. In addition to stone-ground bread and ducks' eggs, we found a local Double Gloucester cheese. My friends and I were discovering that in the ancient world the villages were almost totally self-supporting, and that had been the pattern of human life from the beginning practically. It was a wonderful experience to be living in this basic simplicity, with our needs supplied from the locality. The tragedy of modern times is that we have come to depend on some big city for all our basic necessities.

Back then, too, we had our books, of course — most all of them from the seventeenth or eighteenth century. (We read practically nothing of the nineteenth or twentieth century.) Also, each of us had a beautiful black leather Bible with Gothic letters. We would sit around before breakfast reading our Bibles as literature. We were not interested in religion, specifically, but in literature. The Authorized Version [King James] was, to us, the summit of English literature.

To provide light, we originally thought we would have to have an oil lamp; but once again, Providence took care. We discovered a blacksmith in the neighborhood who made us a beautiful iron candelabra. We used tallow dips for candles. It gave a perfect light. Three or four of us would sit around the table (sometimes there was somebody else staying with us), with our Bibles in front of us.

I went to the Bible three times every day. What made it so fascinating was that we would read the stories of Abraham, Isaac, and Jacob tending their flocks and so on, while there in our neighborhood was a shepherd and his flock. We saw the whole routine of keeping a flock of sheep going on outside our cottage. We thought we were living in the world of the Bible. I often said that you could imagine the Annunciation taking place in that village — a village like that, like Nazareth — something you could not imagine taking place in London or anywhere else.

So this was a time of really getting back to basics, and the Bible had a tremendous impact on us. We read it as literature because literature was something that moved your heart as well as your mind and involved your whole being. And that led us to prayer. I think Hugh was the first one to decide that he would start praying. I hadn't prayed since I was about sixteen. We would kneel on the stone floor in the back of the cottage and pray. I remember reading the *Benedictus:* "Thou child shall be called a prophet of the Most High that will go before the face of the Lord to prepare his way." We had this sense of living in the biblical world. That was decisive.

We also read *The Imitation of Christ,* and that led us to somewhat excessive asceticism. It was Hugh again who instituted it. He thought we should fast on Fridays. I forget exactly what we did, but I think we did have milk and bread. Everything else was cut off. There was a certain austerity growing in my life.

We continued with our reading, and I was especially impressed with Aristotle. I read him in Greek for two or three hours at a time. I didn't gather all the meaning, because I wrestled with the Greek, but it forced itself on my mind. His *Ethics* and *Politics* gave me a real model or basis for life which I had not gotten before at Oxford. It's interesting that

Oxford had built up Aristotle, but his *Metaphysics* was not read there at my time.

Just as the *Ethics* gave me a model basis for life, the *Politics* interested me because Aristotle showed in this work how all ancient people had some sort of kingship. There was always one person, one who was supposed to be a manifestation of God, like the pharaoh, or the emperor of Japan. This person represented the divine order. Then, of course, centuries later the nobles came along — in England we had William the Conqueror — and the Magna Carta of 1216 asserted the nobles' rights. There was nobility in almost all places.

The British development was very interesting. The commoners began to assert their own rights, and by the thirteenth century the English Parliament came into being — with the king, the House of Lords and Nobles, the House of Commons, and the gentry (not the lower classes but only the gentry). That set the pattern for the English Constitution. The climax came in the seventeenth century with the Great Rebellion, after the king kept trying to dominate. While we were at Eastington, I read Clarendon's history of the Great Rebellion, a wonderful book and a wonderful style of writing. This explained a lot for me. I felt here we were living in this world where kings had been overthrown. Aristotle said you go from kingship to the nobles and to democracy and then to dictatorship. Democracy gets out of hand, paving the way for the dictator. That's exactly what was happening in Europe with Mussolini and Hitler during my time.

I went on to read Burke, and I was very impressed. Burke had this deep sense of continuity, of an organic whole. He believed that the state gradually evolves in this way: from kings and nobles and commoners. Then comes the constitution, which is an expression of the organic wholeness of the society. Unfortunately, we have lost all that.

The vision of the world was gradually emerging for us. And for me, especially, the Bible reading began to change everything. It was the Bible that led us to poetry. I think the Book of Job had a tremendous effect on us, and I really felt it was like reading the Greek tragedians, but at a greater depth. They saw that the human drama was not merely a human drama. In Sophocles the gods were in the background, but here you had something much more profound. The Hebrew prophets saw beyond the gods as the cosmic power to the Supreme, an insight that began to penetrate my mind at that time. At the end of the Book of Job, where Job is protesting all this, God appears and asserts himself, and Job says, "I have heard of thee by the hearing of the ear: but now mine eye seeth thee.... Wherefore I abhor myself, and repent in dust and ashes...." Job then realized that he didn't understand anything; and this was a breakthrough, really, of the divine into the human. I felt the same with all the Hebrew prophets. They took you beyond the economic and political order; they saw human life in society move from above. All the tragedies of humanity derive from rebellions against the Supreme Power; and if we lose contact with the Supreme, we cause conflicts and divisions in our world.

So I began to see the modern world as falling away from the divine order and from the law of God and entering more and more into confusion and conflict with dictators and all kinds of tragedy. I saw we were living, in a way, at the center of history; and the Bible offered me a model of how to understand the whole situation — particularly, the assertion of a moral order. And there is a moral order in the universe, not merely an economic or political one. When we neglect the moral order, our politics and economics all go to pieces. We have got to rediscover the moral order. My whole attitude to the present system of civilization was being reinforced by the Bible in a striking way.

Then I came to the New Testament. I expected in reading the gospel seriously for the first time to find a very human Christ; and I think there *is* a very human Christ. But I didn't realize how that human Christ also went beyond humanity and spoke for himself. "No one knows the Father but the Son. No one knows the Son but the Father." How he opened himself to a transcendent mystery, which really was the meaning of life and the meaning of the universe. I began to discover Christ as something more than human and the Church as something more than the human society that I'd always imagined it to be. The Church is really the mystical body of Christ. The Divine present in the human world. That was a great step forward in my understanding.

Saint Paul's understanding of faith came through the imagination. And it was exactly the same for us. For us, the imagination was the power to see through the outer appearance of a thing to its reality. Beauty is Truth, Truth is Beauty. We were trying to find that reality behind. Saint Paul saw through faith. When we go beyond the creative world, beyond the human, we discover the divine mystery at the heart of everything. So that was a wonder, and it is a continuity. Alongside this interest in the Bible, I remained interested in

45

nature and poetry. In fact, I now found in them something deeper and something more meaningful.

After getting into the New Testament, I had to find a church. I discovered that the Church was always there somehow; and we just had to get a link with it again. Fortunately, there was a beautiful fifteenth-century church in Northleach. The curate there, if I recall, was High Church Anglican, and he had all the right ideas. He introduced me to the whole idea of the Church as the tradition coming from the apostles.

Meanwhile, there were ongoing tensions with us at Eastington. We were all different. I was somewhat more austere, Hugh was much more human, and Martyn perhaps stood in between us. We were always arguing and questioning how we should manage our lives. Hugh found it too much of a strain, actually, and he used to go home from time to time. When we went home, it was simply like going into another world altogether. On one visit home Hugh met a girl who would become his wife. After he married, our community broke up. Actually, it was inevitable. So I left and went home again to live for a time.

Eastington certainly changed my life. Though nature and poetry were still the background of my life, they led through the Bible to the discovery of the Christian tradition. The Cotswold world in which we were living was a Christian world. It had beautiful churches and cathedrals, and there was a rhythm to life there. The Coln River ran through our neighborhood, and there was Coln St. Rogers, Coln St. Mary's, and so on. It was there I discovered this Christian life that before I'd only seen depicted in the cathedrals and churches but now I began to see more concretely. So it really changed me from a pagan into a Christian, in a sense, but bringing the paganism into the Church — which is what is needed.

I really discovered myself and my calling as part of this whole world of Christendom.

4

The Dark Night

AFTER LEAVING EASTINGTON, I tried to live a normal life at home, but it was extremely difficult. I had this custom now of fasting. I always found that if I fasted, my prayer and my meditation would grow stronger and stronger. The moment I gave it up, things would begin to disintegrate. I got very thin. People were very anxious, my mother was very worried about it, and this caused tremendous tension.

I decided to return to the Church of England. I took serious steps to study in the theological college and decided to pursue ordination, which gave great joy to my mother. It was very beautiful for a time. I thought I would get ordination in the Church of England. But then I had a rather dramatic experience.

I was on my way to Cuddesdon College in Oxford, which is the theological college. I was riding on my bicycle from Newbury. When I got to the top of the Berkshire Downs, I had been thinking it over and over. I decided that I couldn't stay with the Church of England, even though it was very beautiful of song and had lovely churches.

Unfortunately, perhaps, I had read Newman's *Apologia Pro Vita Sua* when I had returned home from Eastington.

Here was a leading Anglican wrestling with the problem of his church and deciding he had to leave the Church of England for the Church of Rome. Now Rome was a terrible problem — for me and for my family. I always remember my mother saying that nothing would give her greater pain than if anybody she loved should become a Roman Catholic; and my father used to say Roman Catholics are outside the pale. So we never discussed it, really. I remember in our village there was only one Catholic family that we knew of then — we thought of them as odd people. I remember when I was at Magdalen, an undergraduate was pointed out to me as a Roman Catholic, as an oddity. It was actually Father Elwood Sinholm, who later became abbot of Quarr. He and I later became friends; but at that time, any contact was completely outside the range of my thought. It was a very big step to think about the Church of Rome.

Out of curiosity I went down to the church in Newbury to see what it was like, and I was very upset by the service — the whole business of purgatory, and praying for people in purgatory, upset me. The atmosphere was not attractive at all. Then I went to talk to the priest there, using as my standby Hooker's *Ecclesiastical Polity,* which was a Church of England member's understanding of Catholicism, of the Catholic Church, really. It's a beautiful book and gave a wonderful picture of the mystical body of Christ, and that was my ideal of Christianity. This foolish priest immediately tried to put down Hooker and the mystical body, saying it's all up in the air, that the real thing is the Church of Rome. This put me off completely.

While I was riding over to Cuddesdon College I got to the top of the Berkshire Downs, where I decided that I'd put

51

Rome away and go back to the Church of England. The rector at Cuddesdon advised me to go and take time in London in the Bethnal Green Mission.

I think it was a very good idea to spend time in the slums of London and to get back to ordinary life. I remember how all the vegetables in the market there sort of made me feel at home. It was good in its way, but the tension in London was absolutely overwhelming. After living all this time in the Cotswolds, outside the industrial system, to be plunged back into the heart of it was more than I could take. I tried to get some peace of mind. I visited the British Museum to see the Greek sculpture there, and I visited the churches. I went to the National Gallery. But nothing would give me any peace.

One day, while staying at this mission, I went up to my room and decided to spend the night in prayer. This was something absolutely unheard of. I thought prayer was something you would take for two or three hours, maybe, and that you simply fit it into your day. No one spends a whole night in prayer! But it was a big challenge I wanted to take. So I knelt down, and I began to pray. Of course, I struggled against sleep. The worst of all was the struggle against my rational mind. I felt this is "unreasonable." Totally "irrational." Sensible people don't do things like this. I was fighting with the whole conventional world on that side to break with my rational mind and to simply open, really, to a darkness. There was no clear light. The light of reason was gone. But the more I went on, I realized it was my reason that had been the obstacle. I had to break with this rational mind and open to the darkness. There's no light in there.

So I struggled on through the night. I clearly remember I

had a vivid picture of Christ in the Garden of Gethsemane facing darkness and death. This was a real death experience. I think I got up in the morning about seven or eight o'clock. I didn't know what to do. I felt absolutely alone and helpless. Then I heard a voice, not external at all. Something intimated from within: "You must go to a retreat," and I am quite sure I did not know what a retreat was. I'd never been to one or heard of one at all. So I went to the Catholic church where I used to go and asked if there was such a thing as a retreat. The vicar told me that, yes, there was one beginning that day at Westminster House adjoining Westminster Abbey. It was given by the Cowley Fathers, and so I went.

The aftermath of this death experience is difficult to describe. Something simply came over me. The whole world became alive, and I remember the buses in the streets were sort of glowing with light. I could have been run over. I think everything was dissolving. When I went to bed, this sensation was very striking; I felt I could hardly lie down. I would sort of float on the bed. The body seemed to be light and to have lost its heaviness. I picked up a copy of *Dark Night of the Soul* by Saint John of the Cross at that time and read: "I will lead you by a way you do not know to the secret chamber of love." That was amazing. I felt that love, a total love, like a marriage. It was unimaginable how the depth of it simply overwhelmed me. I can only say it was a sort of breakthrough, and the whole place became alive. The crucifix on the wall became alive.

Father Tovey was the retreat master. He was a simple Cowley Father, and he quoted Saint Thomas Aquinas a lot. I thought he was on the right line: He just gave a simple teaching on the Trinity, Incarnation, Redemption, and so on. For me, what he said came as something completely new. I'd been studying it in my own way, but had not fully understood until this moment.

Before I went to pray, I had been reading a book of Bishop Ken, one of the High Church bishops who would not accept the norm. He spoke of the need for repentance, and I didn't know what repentance was. But when I went to the Cowley Fathers, I felt this need for Confession. And for the first time in my life I went to confession. I felt this tremendous repentance, a sense that everything I had done was wrong in some way. I had been like a blind man groping his way when suddenly the light comes. So it was an extraordinary experience. I wept. I had never wept before or since, I think, like that. It cleansed my heart completely. This was an overwhelming conversion experience.

Of course, these are very common experiences. Innumerable people have had these experiences, but each one is always unique. Each one is its own. And that is how it came to me.

5

Catholicism and Benedictine Life

I THOUGHT THINGS would be all right now, but the opposite was true. Once I got back home, the problems got even worse than before. I could not sleep at night. I thought I should be praying instead of sleeping. Then I resumed the fasting. As before, when I fasted, everything seemed to be growing and getting clearer. When I stopped fasting, it all began to disintegrate, and I wondered, "Is the Church of Rome right? Or is the Church of England? Or is Christianity? Or Buddhism?" The whole picture began to disintegrate.

I felt the call again to live in solitude, since everything was getting very confused. I'd been reading Saint Basil and some of the early church fathers. They all spoke of the solitary life. I remembered a very remote place in the Cotswolds where I'd visited when I was living there. So I made my way there and went up through a sort of grove of trees and on to a bare hill. At the top of the hill was a little cottage. Half of it was empty. I took the empty half. A laborer and his wife and children were living in the other half. I settled there. I was trying to leave everything behind again. I was in total confusion now, more so than I was in Eastington. Eastington had been enormously developmental, but now the confusion had all come back.

While I was living in solitude in the Cotswolds, I kept in touch with Michael Cardew. He lived in Winchcombe, in the plain. He would often come and visit, and one day he brought a companion with him, Barbara Millard. She was a girl from South Africa, and we immediately became great friends. She was Anglican, and so was I at that time. We used to go for long walks and visit Anglican churches. She always liked to go in and pay reverence in the church. We shared a lot, and, of course, we also shared our questions about the Church of England. So we developed a very deep friendship. It was the only time I ever thought of marriage, actually, though I don't think it was really that kind of love. It was more a very deep friendship.

She left England and went back to what was then southern Rhodesia and is now Zimbabwe. She married there but was killed in an accident while riding on a horse. Her husband wrote me about it. I had told her once that even if we didn't meet again, our friendship would never cease. I had, I think, the sense then that deep relationships are eternal. I felt that with her.

I had taken only a Bible, a crucifix, a table and chair, and the barest necessities to my modest cottage, where I stayed for several weeks — I don't recall how long exactly. The family supplied me with food, and I lived simply. I spent the time in prayer and study and walks in the hillside, but I could not settle to any sort of permanent way. I kept changing my regime, my times of prayer, and so on. I couldn't get the balance.

Things finally came to a head. I was so confused. I wrote

to Martyn and asked him to come and take me away. I could not manage this anymore. Immediately, as I came to that decision, I suddenly felt that I was missing the point. I had come here to find God, to find my real vocation, but I was just losing it.

So I knelt down to pray. I'll always remember, it was about eight o'clock in the morning, and I decided not to get up until I found an answer to my prayer. I'd never done this before. In the past I had given two hours to prayer or whatever, but then stopped. But this time it was going to be no stop at all. So I simply surrendered to prayer.

It was the most extraordinary event in my life, I think, because I know it was about eight o'clock when I started, and I thought I'd been praying for about two hours; and when I looked at the clock, it was four in the afternoon. So there was a total passing beyond all human experience, really. I don't know what happened, but a message came out absolutely clear: Take work on the farm. Something terribly simple and natural: I was to stay on living on my own, to take work on the farm.

So I took work on the farm, and, day by day, we were working in the fields and going around to the sheep. It was a beautiful experience. The shepherd was a Welshman who knew his Bible, and so we were living in the same world in many ways. I passed the days like that. Then I went down to the bookshop in Wynchcombe, a neighboring town, and I got Newman's *On the Development of Christian Doctrine*. That was decisive, because Newman began that work when he was an Anglican, and he ended it as a Catholic. It was simply the turning point where he discovered that the seed of the gospel had grown from the New Testament, through the fathers, through the history of the Church, like a seed growing into a tree. It had a continuity, from the beginning right up to the present. There have been variations of every kind, of course, but this continuity fully convinced me. So I felt I must join this church. I didn't know anyone. I didn't have a single Catholic friend in the world. I didn't know one Catholic. So I went to the bookshop and asked if there were a Catholic church anywhere, and the man directed me to this monastery. That's where my monastic life began.

I had been prepared for this transition by my reading of Saint Bede, which took place some time before. Just as in the Cotswolds I had seen this religion as the background in the beautiful churches, so, reading Saint Bede, I began to discover that these churches in England — which I thought were part of the Church of England — all stemmed originally from the foundation in Rome. So this again was a revelation. I saw these churches now as part of the much more ancient tradition — from the Bible period, through the early fathers, and spreading all over England and Europe.

Bede became quite a model for me because he had led a very interesting life. He joined a monastery when he was seven years old, and he stayed there for the rest of his life. He was the most learned person in Europe at the time, a wonderful person. So the whole Catholic world, you could say, had in a way come back to me through Bede, and now I was prepared to face it in its concrete reality and it was providential.

I went to this priest and he talked very nicely to me, but he wanted to take me to a monastery. I didn't know that

such things as a monastery existed in the world. We had
been to Tintern and Fountains abbeys. They were all ruins.
I thought this was all of the past and that to find a living
monastery was an amazing thing.

When I discovered this monastery, it was simply extraordinary. It answered all my needs. First of all, it was in a
beautiful natural setting on the hills in the Cotswolds overlooking the plain. It was a beautiful old fifteenth-century
building with some fifteenth-century stained glass. It had
been at one time the country house of the abbot of Gloucester. So I was sort of rejoining the whole tradition there.
Then, in the library, I found all the books I could need.
The prior was Benedict Steuart, a wonderful person. He was
a descendant of the Steuart family and was very proud of
it. He received me with extraordinary understanding. Every
day I would meet with him after dinner at coffee, and we
would talk things over. He fully understood my position and
what I was really seeking after.

The reading had prepared me, and the life at Eastington had set me on the path. Now I could go forward and
actually experience the concrete reality.

Prinknash Abbey had this beautiful setting in the Cotswolds. It was also a wonderful life. Even the white habit
of the monks was tremendously impressive, and the services
in the church were wonderful. It was the old Benedictine
tradition: Divine Office of prayer seven times a day, with
wonderful Gregorian chants. It started with Gregory in the
sixth century and developed until about the ninth century.
We sang this beautiful music day by day, both at prayer
and at the mass, and it sank deep into one's soul. What
tremendously contemplative music! It's a really sacred mu-

sic, something like the sacred music in India. So I think day by day one is being drawn into contemplation, to the experience of God, without always realizing it.

It was also a very human life. There were many lay brothers at the monastery (many of whom were Irish), and they were very good companions. I used to work in the fields and the garden and the shops with all these brothers. That gave a sort of balance to my life, which was very important because it could easily have gotten out of balance. It was a very harmonious life in that regard.

The library was magnificent, and I began some studies. The master of studies was an old Keble scholar who understood my needs. He put me on to Saint Thomas Aquinas, and then he let me go on my own, actually. I absorbed the Catholic faith.

This went on for twenty-five years almost without a break. The instability, conflict, and confusion were all brought to an end through the stable background of a normal human life and daily manual work. I did every kind of manual task in the garden and in the fields, as well as in the stone quarry — breaking stones, mixing concrete, even helping to plaster and build. I did all this with the brothers, and it was very positive activity. The studies went on in the same way, too, and everything was integrated in prayer.

Prayer simply encompassed the whole monastic life; and it was beautifully arranged. We had the early morning prayer (Matins and Lauds), which began at four o'clock. Before it ended — particularly on Sundays, when it was rather long — the sun was beginning to rise. And the dawn came with the birds singing outside. Then at six o'clock we would have the first hour of the day in the Roman reckoner* (Prime). At nine o'clock, the third hour of the day, we would have the Office of Terce, followed by the Eucharist. The Eucharist was celebrated with great beauty — the vestments, the candles, the incense, and the singing. It's all enchanting when there's a genuine spirit behind it; but, of course, it can become empty of meaning if you're not careful.

The sixth-hour session (Sext) began at twelve o'clock, and the ninth hour (None) at three o'clock. Vespers were in the evening at six o'clock. *Completorium* (Compline) would complete the day. We always sang this in the dark, the same psalms every night beginning with: "He who abides under the shelter of the Most High...." With just two candles burning in the sanctuary, all was dark; so it was beautiful. It created a special atmosphere of prayer that I think is the main thing.

I absorbed the Catholic doctrine rather uncritically — or perhaps that's a little unfair to say. I absorbed what was then the critical understanding of the Church. It was rather limited, but it was meaningful because it was all taken up into this atmosphere of prayer so that the sacrament and doctrine were entwined in a deeper life of contemplation.

I was learning contemplation, though I must emphasize even though we had half an hour of meditation after Vespers every day, we had no method of meditation. Saint Benedict didn't give any. So we let our minds wander, I think. Sometimes we did get some experience of genuine prayer, but obviously there was a real weakness in having no proper method of prayer to discipline the mind and to open it to the

---

*breviary (the Divine Office at that time)

deepest level of union with God. That I learned afterward, when I learned how to say the mantra from a Benedictine monk who had been taught the practice.

I think I learned to trust in Divine Providence, probably for the first time, when I went to Farnborough Abbey as prior of the community there. At Prinknash Abbey I was just one of the monks and everything was provided for me. But as prior, I was responsible for the community. There were about thirty monks, and we had a total fixed income of five hundred pounds a month. It was not nearly sufficient for the community. We had to find ways of managing. And we learned to trust in Divine Providence to provide what was necessary. We lived month by month.

I always recall one time when we reached our limit. We had an overdraft at the bank, and it was at its limit. Some sisters wrote us from Africa saying they wanted a cow, and could we help them. The community decided to make a venture of faith. I remember talking it over with the monks then. We simply said we would "trust God." Then I wrote the sisters, saying, "Yes, we'll send you the money for the cow...." I think it was the next day that the money came for what we wanted. So little things like that convince you, in time, that there is a Providence. We have to depend on our own resources all the time, but I think every act of genuine faith, like that, teaches us that there is an overriding Providence. I've seen it go on ever since. In our ashram in India we always have lived from month to month, as well. We have never had a fixed income. But always, somehow, it has come.

While I was at Kurisumala, there was a lady in America — a retired teacher — who had been sending money for charity. We had no resources, really, but we had a farm. So we did use the money for charity. When we came here [to Saccidananda in Tamil Nadu] — I told her that we were very grateful for her gifts for charity, but now *we* really needed money for ourselves. From that time onward she sent us a check for five hundred dollars two or three times a year. And that is what kept the whole community going for about five years. After she died, somebody else came along. Still, although something has always come, we basically lived from month to month. That teaches one to trust.

Learning to trust — that is the great thing. You realize that you do have to do your work, you have to provide what you can, but also you have to learn to believe that Providence is going to provide all that you really need. One learns to trust like that, day by day. Of course, it does not mean that you just sit down and wait for things to happen. You have to do something, and you do what you need to do, in the belief that Providence is working in and through you, not that you alone are responsible. It is so difficult for us to know that.

In the gospels we read, "Seek first the kingdom of God." Many people have a long list of desires and wants and think that the kingdom of God will come and satisfy these needs. I believe that the reverse is true. We have to let go of our demands and our needs and our personal desires and allow Providence to work. Providence teaches you to do what is necessary, and so you do what is necessary. You are always in the hands of something beyond yourself. That is the secret of trust, really.

For twenty-five years I had such stability, having taken a vow of stability: to be in the same place, doing the same thing, eating the same food, and living with the same people. It may sound terribly monotonous, but it was enriched with all this beauty of ritual and charm, meditation and reading, and community life.

I must mention that after I was professed — following a year of philosophy, a year of novitiate, three years of profession, then solemn profession in 1936 and ordination in 1940 — I was made guest master. We had some guests — not a great many: six or a dozen at most. Every week people came, and I met all sorts of people — some very learned, some leading Catholic thinkers, and lots of ordinary people. People with all kinds of provenance, which they brought with them to the monastery. We could talk things over in an atmosphere of prayer. We really didn't have simple answers for everything, but we wanted to let people experience the prayer that would open their hearts to what God would teach them. That was wonderful, really. I made so many friends then.

C. S. Lewis came to visit me when I was a monk at Prinknash Abbey. While he was talking to me, he realized that I was under a vow of obedience. He also had a talk with the prior when he was there. I cannot remember exactly what he said, but he felt that the prior must have a pretty difficult time with me, with the strength of my ego, which was going to be a real problem. Of course, living under the vow of obedience was a tremendous help at the time. I think it can become dangerous later on, but at a certain stage, to learn simply to do what other people tell you is really valuable. It stops you from centering on the ego and gets you out of it. I think you have to reach a more mature period before your ego really goes. Then you do things from your own initiative; they don't come from your ego anymore. They come from a deeper center within. That's the difference.

I remained at Prinknash about fifteen years or so. Then in 1947 we were offered a monastery [St. Michael's Abbey] in Farnborough, which is in Hampshire. It belonged to a French congregation [Solesmes] who were giving it up, and they asked us to take it over. I was sent there as the prior at that time, and it was a good experience. The abbey was a beautiful place with a strange history. When Napoleon III lost the Franco-Prussian War, he came to England, first to Kent, then to Farnborough. The emperor and the empress had their house on one hill, and they built this church on the opposite hill, in a beautiful Baroque style. We wore velvet vestments that had been made from the empress's garments. The emperor and empress, as well as the prince imperial, were all buried in the crypt underneath. So being there was a kind of historic event for me. Though I remained for only four or five years, it was a very good experience.

Then the community was offered a site in Scotland,* near Elgin. It was a thirteenth-century monastery that had been kept and preserved to some extent. Now it has been almost completely renovated, and the community has flourished. In fact, there are a good many monks there now.

---

*at Pluscarden

6

The Journey to India

I THINK the person most responsible for my going to India was Toni Sussman. She was one of Jung's first six disciples. She and her husband, who was a Jew, came to England in the time of Hitler and settled in London. She was a Jungian analyst and had a practice in psychotherapy and meditation. Her library was filled with books on Eastern spirituality, and she really opened up to me the whole Indian world. Gradually, Yoga and Vedanta took on a central place in my life.

While studying and pursuing that direction, I met Father Benedict Alapatt, an Indian Benedictine monk from Kerala in southern India. He had joined the Monastery of Saint André in Belgium, but he wanted to start a foundation in India. I believe he wrote to all the monasteries in Europe, and I was the only one who replied. We became friends and agreed (got permission, actually) to go to India together. The year was 1955.

I had another great friend, Dr. Allan, who, like Toni Sussman, was a Jungian analyst. She had been a friend for years and had helped me in many ways. She paid my fare to India. (When she died some time later, she left me three thousand pounds in her will. That three thousand pounds, which was about fifty thousand rupees, actually paid for all the original buildings in Shantivanam.)

As far as I can remember, there were no flights to India at that time, so we went by a steamship: the *Chu San* — one of the last, I think. It was a beautiful experience sailing down through the Straits of Gibraltar, then on to Port Said. Port Said was my introduction to the East. We went ashore to see the people. It was a totally different world there — particularly with the children. The boys and girls were so spontaneous. What first struck me, and has ever since, was the beauty of the human body — what Blake called the "human form divine." In the East nakedness is normal, and a person wears clothes not from convention but from necessity; but they still retain their natural state. In the West, though, nakedness is unnatural: We have to be clothed and may only occasionally remove our clothing. But in Port Said I took another step in getting back to nature. It was another breakthrough, as it really opened me up to the East.

We then sailed down the Red Sea, with Mount Sinai not so very far off in the distance. From there we continued the journey into Bombay. Bombay was sort of a world of the heart's desire for me. I was enchanted with it. I think I'd probably be less so now, but the whole Oriental atmosphere — the women in saris, the men wearing turbans, and the natural spontaneous movements — is so fascinating. I used to say that people in the East live from the unconscious, while we Westerners live more from the conscious. Their movements are more spontaneous, like those of birds and animals; our movements are deliberate. There is great beauty in that, and so I was really enchanted. We went to the churches in Bombay — they were Western churches, with Western altars and

Western vestments — which were very crowded. People pack themselves into these churches — along the windows, in the aisles, and everywhere — causing something of a chaos. Yet, seeing it all, I saw a beauty and spontaneity.

I spent about a fortnight in Bombay, and then we went on to Poona, which is a sort of theological center in India. That was a good experience for me, too. We then traveled to Bangalore, where the archbishop welcomed us. I stayed at the clergy house by the cathedral with Father Alapatt, and there I met Dr. Raymond Panikkar. I wanted to learn Sanskrit, and we found a wonderful Sanskrit teacher, a Carmelite sister, who held an M.A. degree in Sanskrit from Benares — first in her class. She was brilliant. I learned only the basics. Father Alapatt got right ahead almost immediately, which was extraordinary. But at least I learned the basics. We also went to a Hindu pundit (a Sanskrit expert and scholar). So we received a very good grounding in Sanskrit.

We also toured Mysore and saw the temples there — Halebid and Somnathpur and so on. It reminded me of the cathedrals in England: marvelous architecture, and always, behind it all, this life of the spirit.

When I was in Bombay, we went to see the Caves of Elephanta, which are caves hollowed out of the rock, and we marveled at the beautiful sculptures of the figure of Shiva with his three faces. One side is the gentle face, the loving aspect. The other is the fierce face, the angry aspect. And in the center is the face of contemplative wisdom. This really showed me that behind all the beauty of the external is the real spirit of India, this contemplative wisdom. These people are absorbed in God, just as Shiva's face is totally absorbed in God. I felt that I had really touched the heart of India when I saw that sculpture. It gave me a profound sense of the sacred in India: the sacredness of the earth and the land. The sacredness of the cow. I'll never forget being beside the river once and seeing a little *lingam* and *yoni,* the male and female organs, just set down there. This scene reinforced for me the sacredness of sex. This sacred sense is deep in India, and so is the sense of the feminine, the Mother. The cow is the Mother, the earth is the Mother. We are always related to Mother Nature, to Mother Earth. And this is a beautiful experience.

While we were visiting the temples in Mysore, we met a man in one town who invited us to his home. It was a tiny little cottage, where he lived with his wife and three children. One child was lying sick, and the others were play-ing and singing. He was a musician. We sat in that little house of utter poverty and simplicity, and they sang these beautiful songs in Sanskrit and other Indian languages, all sacred songs. The father sang with the children. The mother brought us tea in little vessels, and then she joined in the singing. As they were all singing these sacred songs, I felt that there, in that little tiny hut, in that little village, I was living at the heart of Indian culture. It was one more instance of initiation into this different world.

Soon after we arrived in Bangalore, we began to look for some place to found an ashram. We found a place about twelve miles away, near a village called Kengeri. There we bought a little bungalow, and we furnished it very simply. But at that time we were still living in a very Western man-ner. I had a Western Benedictine habit, I wore shoes and socks, and we had tables and chairs and spoons and forks. We thought it was very simple, but it was still Western. We built a little chapel — but again, in a Western style — even though we had the *Upanishads,* the [*Bhagavad*] *Gita,* and other Eastern things. Young students began to come up from the village, and when they found that we knew the *Upanishads* and the *Gita* much better than they did, they were tremendously impressed. They said they'd never known a Christian like us. What was interesting, though, was that they would simultaneously ask for a life of Christ. That taught me that if you are open to other people's religions, they will open themselves to yours; but you have to take the initiative, really. So that was a wonderful beginning.

We lived a very simple life in Kengeri. There were four of us, two Indians having now joined us. One of them was a very charming man from Kerala, but a little disturbing. One day he left. Then he returned one morning at four o'clock when we were at prayer. He took all our watches, fountain pens, and whatever he could lay his hands on, and carried them off. We eventually found him. (And I visited him in prison later on.)

Kengeri was a good experience in its way, but, for various reasons, we couldn't stay there. Then I met Father Francis Mahieu, who had been a Cistercian monk. He was also searching for an ashram in India, so he and I joined together and went to Kerala, while Father Alapatt went on to another ashram. The year was 1958.

In Kerala there are both the Latin and the Syrian rites. Actually, there are two Syrian rites. We joined the west Syrian, partly because it was the only Catholic church there where, if I recall, the liturgy was in the vernacular — in this case Malayalam — and it was a beautiful liturgy. We accepted the liturgy and planned to build our monastery, or ashram.

72

Unfortunately, the work was delayed, and we had to stay in a palm leaf hut until the ashram was built. The building was so delayed that the monsoon came on before we were ready. The monsoon is something serious: It can rain about 250 inches during a period of about two or three months — June, July, and August. This one was just a deluge. We had to put planks down to sleep on because the straw got so wet. Everything was wet. Then the sun would come out, and we'd put everything out in the sun to dry — before it started all over again.

We celebrated all the Syrian liturgies in this hut, complete with incense, prayers and singing, and everything else that was required. Finally, the ashram was ready, and we moved in.

Father Francis and I led a very regular monastic life. The Cistercians are somewhat stricter than the Benedictines — but that was good. We began wearing the *kavi*, the traditional dress of Indian monks. Father Francis had come to India long before I did, and he had learned the Indian ways at another ashram. So he introduced me to the *kavi*, and together we began to adopt normal Indian customs — like sitting on the floor, sleeping on a mat, eating with the hands, and so on. So all that was introduced to me in the Kurisumala Ashram in Kerala. Since we had taken on the Syrian liturgy, I chose to learn Syriac — which I found very easy for some reason.

Over time we had built a nice little community. Some came and some went, but in the end there must have been about twelve of us. We also had a very fine herd of cows. Father Francis was Flemish and had farming blood. He developed a beautiful pedigree Jersey herd. We began to supply milk to the neighborhood, and eventually other people got cows. This was a very creative period in its way.

Our library had a stove, partly to keep our books dry and partly to warm us — especially during the monsoon when the rain poured down. I used to sit by the stove while I translated the Syriac. I even gave classes to the students there, because it was a well-stocked library, which included the Bible, the writings of the church fathers, and so on. This creative period lasted for ten years.

Father Francis had already spent a year or two at Shantivanam Ashram in Tamil Nadu before we met. The little hut he had built there still remains. He had gone to Shantivanam originally because he had a link with the two French priests — Father Le Saux and Father Monchanin — who had founded it in 1950. Shantivanam represented the first movement of the Church in India to live a Christian life according to the customs of a Hindu Ashram — with all its simple ways and customs that are part of life in the village.

Father Francis had decided to leave Shantivanam because he felt that his students would not get vocations in Tamil Nadu and that vocations were in Kerala. He first came to Kerala to learn Sanskrit, but he was so charmed with the life there, and particularly the Syrian liturgy, that he decided to start the Kurisumala Ashram in Kerala and adopt the local customs.

Then Father Monchanin died in 1957, and Father Le Saux went to the north and settled in a hermitage in the Himalayas. He tried to keep up Shantivanam, but it was too much to keep coming and going. Finally, he decided to leave it altogether and asked Father Francis to take over. But since he had been in Kurisumala so long, we had to decide which of us would remain and which of us would come to Shantivanam. (I had been in Kurisumala for ten years with Father Francis, who was in charge, and we got on extremely well.) Father Francis wanted to stay in Kerala, so of course I came here [to Shantivanam] in 1968 with two monks from Kurisumala. I don't choose what I have to do; it happens to me always by providence.

We started from scratch, with practically nothing — just a few little huts, a little chapel, a tiny little library, and just the three of us. From the Syrian liturgy we gradually developed an Indian liturgy, which has continued to the present. Then we gradually transformed the church itself, making it into a real temple with a beautiful *vimana** on the top. We had to built up the ashram from its original two or three huts. We gradually increased the number of huts and built a guest house for six people. And it kept growing. Now we can accommodate about forty people.

We decided to build a beautiful library to replace the tiny one that existed. It's important to know that the library and all the buildings were built by local craftsmen. We never used anybody from outside. The same is true for the *vimana* — we found a local craftsman who was accustomed to building *vimanas* on the temples; but instead of the traditional Hindu gods, we had him make individual statues of the Virgin Mary, Saint Peter, Saint Paul, and Saint Benedict.

This *vimana* is built over the sanctuary, and there's a deep significance to that. In the sanctuary is the altar, the altar of sacrifice, death, and resurrection, when we ascend to the heavenly world. First come the four living creatures of the

---

*A dome, usually found on the top of a Hindu temple, with gods and goddesses.

75

Apocalypse, whose cosmic powers are ruling the world, and then is the communion of the saints, the Virgin Mary, Saint John, Saint Peter, Saint Paul, and Saint Benedict. The dome above is the heavenly sphere and points to the beyond. So you are positioned right at the base of death and resurrection to the final stage. This has deep symbolic significance.

We established our liturgy in the church, and it simply grew gradually. It is very interesting: Nothing was planned ahead, but people came and introduced one thing or another and it grew. We always begin with Sanskrit chanting. That is very important: It is a sacred language and has a beauty and a power. We always chant the Gayatri Mantra, the most sacred mantra in the *Vedas*. Then we normally have a Sanskrit hymn, followed by readings from the different scriptures. That has been a very important part of the liturgy. We read from the *Vedas,* the *Upanishads,* and the *Bhagavad-Gita;* also the *Dharmmapadda* of the Buddha and the *Tao te ching.* Then, especially in the evening, we read the devotional poets, like Manikka's *Tiru-vasaham,* the great Tamil mystic Kabir, and other saints. We open ourselves to all the religious traditions of the world.

Then we go on to the psalms and other Bible reading, as well as some reading from the church fathers. We do what is called "Bhajan" singing, chants in different Indian languages that are taken up by all the people and then repeated and repeated. It's a very joyous thing, accompanied by drums and cymbals. We have a really joyful liturgy. We always end with *ārati,* which is the Hindu way of worship. This involves waving lights before the holy place. I discovered the meaning of that when I went to the Temple Shrungam in Trichy and the *pujari* took me into the inner sanctuary. There is a beautiful figure there of Vishnu reclining; the *pujari* took a torch and waved it in front of the statue to bring it to light. God is in the darkness, too, so we take the light and bring God to light, as it were. Then we take the light to our eyes. So having every prayer end with this *arrati* is very deeply meaningful.

We also still took the *kavi,* or saffron-colored robes, which we had in Kerala. The *kavi* is material dyed with a natural dye, reddish in color — really an earth color, the color of fire — and it is quite significant. It is a sign of *Sannyasa,* which means total surrender to God beyond all form, names, images, concepts — beyond all religion, in a sense. A religion is the organization of the spiritual life, but the spirit itself is beyond religion. Religion belongs to a world of signs, of sacraments; and they are necessary — you cannot do without them. But we must go through them and beyond them. *Sannyasi* is a sign that we divest ourself of all clothing, go into the water, and "die." Then we are reborn and are clothed in the *kavi.*

The symbolism of the *kavi* is that you burn up all the limitations and sins of the world, and you are clothed in the fire. It was said at baptism, "He will baptize you in the Holy Spirit and with fire." This ritual takes the form of a baptism in that you go under the water and you are reborn. You put on the *kavi,* and you are clothed with the spirit and with fire. It is a wonderful ceremony and still remains a basic custom of the ashram.

❖

It has been quite a traumatic story. I came here [to Shantivanam] with two monks from Kurisumala, but problems began immediately with one of them. I would not like to judge him, but he certainly did not get on with me. After less than a year, I think, he elected to go back to Kurisumala. The other one was a good monk. We sent him to study philosophy and theology, and he did very well. But at the end of his studies, he elected to marry — and so he left us.

I was left alone for maybe two or three years, with no permanent members at all. Then a Tamil named Stephen — whom I had known since coming to India — joined the ashram to work with me. He had been a devoted disciple of Father Monchanin, and when he came to me he made me, his guru. For years he sort of followed my ideas.

Stephen was a very dynamic character, and you never quite knew what he was going to do next. He brought his wife and two small children, and for five years or so they really managed the ashram. He was a very capable business manager; and since he was a Tamil, he knew all the local people. His wife was very supportive, and the two children were charming. It was a beautiful arrangement, and it worked until two new monks came, who really began to form the ashram. Though Stephen didn't want the monks to take over, they did; and he had to separate. He and his wife left the ashram to be run by the new monks.

Fathers Amaldas and Christudas arrived from Kurisumala quite out of the blue. Amaldas came and prostrated himself at my feet and said he wanted to be with me. He was a wonderful person, a very simple Kerala Catholic. He had learned Yoga at a fairly early age in Kurisumala. He had several Yoga teachers and himself became an absolute master yogi, being called to give Yoga courses in Europe and America and Australia. And he wrote two books on Yoga. He was a really wonderful disciple, and we had hopes he would take over the ashram in time; but he died rather suddenly of a heart attack.

Before the monks' arrival, though many people came and went, there was no settlement in the ashram at all for many years. One trusted in Divine Providence the whole time, really. You weren't expecting things to happen regularly at all. If somebody came, we welcomed them; if they left, we had to accept that. I think that is the only way to be, really.

The interesting thing is that the ashram grew sort of spontaneously. Every person who came contributed something to the liturgy, to the prayer, to our way of life, and that's how the whole thing grew. It's hard to explain. But it has continued right to the present day. That, to me, is the Great Principle: to allow things to grow. We always tend to want to construct and impose, to organize, to build the proper monastery, and all the rest of it. With this one, it's just been allowed to grow. That is the principle of the Tao. Never impose anything. Stand back and let the Tao work, the great order of the universe. That is an excellent principle, and the one that really allowed the ashram to grow.

We did, of course, have many, many problems. Some people who came were very bad — we had a good many drug addicts coming at times. I always recall one of them telling me, "I also am seeking God." These people, very often, were good people — but had given up the conventional life, were searching for some deeper meaning, and they found in drugs the way to take them up to a high. But, of course, drugs let you down afterward. So many problematic people came, but we made a rule never to refuse anybody. I think it's important to learn to accept people without necessarily having them leave. They leave of themselves. They find, after a time at the ashram, that it is not their way.

❖

At Kurisumala, as I've mentioned, we had taken the Syrian rite and became members of the Syrian Church (so we had no status in the Latin Church). That meant I had to change my *stabilitas,* as we call it, from my monastery in England to Kurisumala Ashram. However, when I came to Shanti-vanam, where there was no Syrian rite, I had to change again — to the Latin rite. I went back to the Benedictine tradition because we had to find some status in the Church. This had caused a great problem with Father Francis.

I was keen on an oblate status. An oblate is a spiritual bond but not a juridical one.* I felt it left me the freedom to develop, in my own way, within the tradition, but without being bound by canon law. I even went so far as to ask the abbot primate,† who was a good friend then and is now an archbishop, whether he would accept the community as an oblate community.

He said there were too many people wanting to be under him, and he did not feel that he could do it. So that was a big problem. Father Francis really wanted the community to be under Kurisumala, which would have meant under the Syrian jurisdiction. But that would not have given us the freedom we both wanted, and caused some friction for years. It was a real problem.

---

*i.e., with some of the canonical restrictions.
†Dom Rembert Weakland.

The other problem was with the local bishop. He had come from the Fisher community in Tamil Nadu where Saint Francis Xavier had converted the people. It is a very strong community, three hundred years old, and with a very deep faith. But these are very emotional people and will easily take a side of one against another. The bishop did not like foreigners, and he did not like Malayalis. Since I was a foreigner and my two disciples were Malayalis, from Kerala, there was certain friction.

Then we adopted this Indian style of life and Indian liturgy. An Indian liturgy was approved for the Church in India by the bishops. Their center for this is located in Bangalore, and is the national center. But many of the bishops in Tamil Nadu did not approve of this at all. They wanted their own liturgy, and several times our bishop tried to prevent us from using our liturgy. I would write to the commission in Bangalore and they would write back and say, "You have an ashram. You have the freedom to use this Indian liturgy." Only then would the bishop accept it; but it was a source of constant conflict and made things very awkward. Fortunately, he came around in the end — particularly when we joined the Camaldolese.*

That was a very important step. We had no status: We did not belong to the Syrian Church, and we had no place in the Latin Church. Then a monk from the Camaldolese came and stayed a year with us. He was delighted with our life and took the news back to the Camaldolese, and they offered to let us join their congregation. So in 1980 I

*The Camaldolese is a branch of the larger Benedictine community, founded by Romuald, an Italian nobleman turned monk, around 1023. The Camaldolese trace their spiritual lineage back to the early desert fathers and mothers as well as to earlier ascetics and Christ himself. Camaldolese combine the eremitical life with community life.

was admitted to the congregation of Camaldolese as a Benedictine monk. Two years later the whole community was accepted. That gave us a status in the Church. At the same time, they were very open to the ashram spirit. They did not want to change our way of life, they accepted our habit and all the rest of it, and at the same time gave us a status as monks of Camaldolese. This brought a tremendous relief.

So the conflict with Father Francis and the bishop was resolved. The bishop was particularly delighted to have these monks of Camaldolese in his diocese. He came to ordain Fathers Amaldas and Christudas, in the course of time. All those wounds were healed in the end, but it had been a painful period. At the same time, though, growth was taking place. When Amaldas and Christudas were finally professed and when they were finally ordained, the community was fully established, and it's gone on from there.

It took a long wait — but mind you, in a sense, all these things are rather subsidiary to me. We came to start a contemplative community. We realized that to fit it into the structures of the Church was not going to be easy, and we would just have to be patient until the thing would work.

Today there is still a very big problem in the Church in India. There are many people, particularly sisters, who feel this call to contemplative life, and they want to take *Sannyasis*. They want to live the ashram style of life, with the freedom of the spirit, the customs of India. Their religious congregations are often open to it in many ways. They send their sisters now to us for retreats and so on. But it's very difficult to fit it into their constitutions. They are not organized for this kind of life, and so it becomes a real problem. Some sisters have to leave their congregation in order to live a more authentic spiritual life. Others try to find a way to fit it into their congregation. It's a paradox in a sense, and it is still not resolved.

I think the Camaldolese have been the most successful. We have been able to fit in as monks of Camaldolese, but still keep the freedom of the spirit which the ashram demands. So in that way we have been blessed. But it has taken time to reach that point — all these things take time. One just has to be patient, to allow things to unfold — that's how I always see it.

In regard to feeling lonely, I have always felt that it was not my work but the work of God; and I really trusted in that. Also, I have had extraordinary support. Father Benedict Alapatt, the Benedictine monk with whom I came to India, was well known in India. He knew many of the bishops, so I was accepted from the beginning.

When we went to Kerala, the bishops there were extremely friendly and fully accepted us. Even when we came here to Shantivanam, although the bishop was a little hostile in his way, the acceptance was very great, and people began to come. Though I should say, it was interesting at first. We would get priests and our brothers from Kerala and from abroad, but very little from Tamil Nadu. However, that gradually changed: Now we have as many from Tamil Nadu as anywhere else. Things take time, but I have always had support, so I have never felt lonely, really, not seriously.

❖

It is wonderful to reflect back on how Father Monchanin had this dream in the 1930s in Europe of an Indian Benedictine ashram and how it took fifty years for that dream to become realized. But step by step, with many setbacks and feelings of failure, the thing gradually emerges. I think what one learns is not to be upset by apparent failures and worried by a lack of success but to see that the whole movement of nature is so complex. It is the Tao, you see, this rhythm. You have to learn to fit into the rhythm and allow it to carry you, and then it carries you forward in the end. That is the thing. Then you get confidence that something is guiding. I have that strong feeling: that the ashram has been guided from the beginning, from the time of Monchanin onward. There has always been a Providence at work, and people feel it today. Many attribute it to me, but I don't think it's so. I think there is something far beyond that, working in the ashram, drawing it toward the ideal which Father Monchanin conceived and which we have been trying to follow and which the Church in India is really looking for. Now, more and more, it is being accepted. The Church in Rome does now accept this whole idea of enculturation and dialogue. They are the two fundamentals now in the mission of the Church with regard to other religions. The method is dialogue. We don't simply try to impose; we try to listen, to learn, to understand.

I feel that India gave me the other half of my soul. My life in England, first of all, was dominated by the intellect, by the rational mind. I went from school to college and I passed exams in Latin and Greek, and so on. I was always searching to get beyond the mind. Of course, D. H. Lawrence and the Romantic poets, such as Wordsworth, were opening this world to me. But whereas that was something rare in England, in India it was the norm — the natural order of society.

The earth, the air, and the water: They were all sacred, and the human being is sacred.

In the beautiful gesture, *namaste,* we worship God in each person as we greet them, really. I think I can say that I was discovering the feminine because the masculine mind dominates in Europe and was dominating my mind. The feminine is the intuitive, the sensitive, and also the sensual mind — in a sense, the whole bodily life. Christianity tends to put this down; India has accepted it totally. In India it is all integrated: the sensual and the spiritual. I still go on discovering that other half all the time.

7

The Stroke –
Discovering the Feminine

ON JANUARY 25, 1990, I was sitting meditating, as I usually do at six o'clock, on the verandah of my hut; and suddenly, without any warning, a terrific force came and hit me on the head. It seemed like a sort of sledgehammer. Everything seemed like a television screen before the picture is focused. Just everything was like this. Then this force seemed to be dragging me out of the chair. It was coming from the left and pulling me out of my chair. It came suddenly, absolutely unexpected, without any warning. It was very scary, really. I managed to crawl onto the bed. I think I was breathing very heavily. Christudas came about an hour afterward. I lost count of time. He found me there, and then the news went around.

For the next week, I'm told, I didn't speak at all. I can't recall anything in detail. I don't know what happened during that week. There was a period of blankness. Then I began to come around. I woke up one night at about one o'clock, and I thought I was going to die. Everybody thought I was going to die. I decided to prepare for death, so I said the prayers, the normal prayers, and invoked the angels and so on, and waited for death. Nothing happened. Then, after an hour or two, Christudas came along and massaged me, and I began to get back to normal.

I had some breakfast, and then I felt sort of restless, disturbed, not knowing quite what was happening. The inspiration came suddenly again to surrender to the Mother. It was quite unexpected: "Surrender to the Mother." And so somehow I made a surrender to the Mother. Then I had an experience of overwhelming love. Waves of love sort of flowed into me. Judy Walter, my great friend, was watching. Friends were watching beside me all the time. I called out to her, "I'm being overwhelmed by love."

It was an extraordinary experience. Psychologically, I think, it was the breakthrough to the feminine. I was very masculine and patriarchal and had been developing the *animus,* the left brain, all this time. Now the right brain — the feminine, the phonic power, the earth power — came and hit me. It opened up the whole dimension of the feminine, of the earth, and so on. When I thought of surrendering to the Mother, it was certainly Mary, because I often say the "Hail Mary," but also it was more the Black Madonna that came into my mind. The mother who is mother of the earth as well as the heavens — Mother Nature, as a whole. I also thought of my own mother, and motherhood in general.

This was really the opening of a totally new dimension to me. I can see how growing up in a patriarchal society, and living all this time so much from the intellect, this [other] side had been suppressed. Now it simply came up like this. It was very violent at first, like something that hits you on the head; but then it is extremely loving. It comes and embraces you. So this was a wonderful experience, and it's gone on ever since.

What I understood this to mean, after a time, was that the left brain and the whole rational system had been knocked down, and the right brain and the intuitive understanding, the sympathetic mind, had been opened up. The left brain keeps going all the time, but the right brain is always in control. I got this sense of *advaita,* nonduality. The divisions between things broke away, and everything was flowing into everything else.

Today I still see the divisions, but I feel differently about people and things: It's all one, in a sense. And I have never lost the sense that all the diversities are contained in the one. This has become more and more my understanding.

Advaita does not mean "one" in the sense of eliminating all differences. The differences are present in the one in a mysterious way. They are not separated anymore, and yet they are there. To me, this is extremely important. When we go to a deeper level of consciousness, we should not lose the diversity of things and their individuality. On the contrary, the diversity, the multiplicity, is taken up into the unity. It cannot be put into words properly, and it cannot be explained rationally. It is simply an experience of *advaita.* The more one reads from the Hindu or the Buddhist or the Taoist or the Christian mystics, the more one realizes that this nonduality has been the great discovery beyond the rational mind with all its dualities of good and evil, light and darkness, black and white, conscious and unconscious, male and female. All these divisions are there, but they are contained in a unity. That is the important thing.

The Tibetan Dzogchen, which I came across fairly recently, I think puts it more profoundly than anywhere else: We all have a deep sense that the whole multiplicity of being

90

is contained in the unity of the one, in this nondual relationship — not one, and not two. Personally, I have taken this
(and it came gradually) to be a sign of the Trinity. The God,
in the Christian sense, is not a person. We tend to project
an image of the Father, or of Christ, or something, but these
are projections. Beyond all the projections, the Father is simply the ground, the source, the origin. He is the one beyond
name, beyond form. From the one comes the self-expression,
the self-revelation, the self-manifestation of the one. That
is the Word — the Word that expresses the Father as the
source.

This idea comes through very much in the work of Meis-
ter Eckhart. In that Word is contained the whole universe.
When the Father expresses himself in his Word, the whole
of creation is present in the universe — you and I, the trees
and the earth, the sun and the stars. Everything is contained
in that one Word, in its nondual reality. It's not simply one;
the Father and the Son are not a monad. If they were simply one, that would not be an identity. Rather, it is union in
relationship.

The Trinity comes to me now as a key to the understanding of life. From the Father — the source, the origin,
the *sunyata,* the abyss of being, the void, the emptiness,
the darkness — comes forth the Word — the wisdom, the
light, the sun. It is a nondual relationship. The Son is not
the Father, the Father is not the Son. They are not separate, either; it's neither one nor two. It is what is called a
subsistent relationship. This is a key to life, because today
we see the whole universe in terms of this interdependent
relationship.

In the physical universe and the psychological universe,

we are all members of this whole, in which each is an integral element; all interwoven, interdependent, distinct, and yet one. So the Son reveals the Father, the abyss, and manifests all that is latent in the godhead. All the seeds of creation are present there. And in the Son those seeds come to life. The whole of creation is mirrored in the Son, and all time and space, and you and I, and every detail of human existence is already present in that one reality. That is why Saint Paul could say he [Christ] knew us in him before the foundation of the world. We all come from this depth of the abyss beyond. Then comes this Word — the "ideas," as Plato would say — and the whole of creation is present in the Word. The "ideas" come into manifestation through the Spirit. The Spirit is the *Shakti,* the energy of the divine power, and it is what propels the whole universe. When we speak of the great "Big Bang," the beginning of creation, it is simply the "ideas" and the Word being manifested through this power of the Spirit. The *Shakti* manifests the whole of creation, and then it comes out into space and time. I really see the Trinity as a key to understanding this profoundly.

Interestingly, the founder of Saccidananda Ashram, Father Monchanin, once said that our aim is *advaita* and the Trinity: nonduality and the Trinity. They are often opposed, of course. Many think of *advaita* as monism, in that it sort of removes all differences; and then the Trinity becomes three solid persons, all separated. But really it is a nondual mystery.*

All this experience and insight have really only emerged

---

* "diversity in unity," as Bede often described it.

since my stroke. From that time I have gone on reflecting over it, and the experience continues. In a way, I never feel separated from the earth or the trees or people or whatever. It is all one, and yet the differences remain. This is so important.

The danger of *advaita* is that it tends to minimize the universe, and even to deny it. It is *maya,* an illusion, or it is just a play, not taken seriously. In this true *advaita* everybody and everything has its own unique reality; but the divine reality is present in every plant, every animal, every atom, every proton. The divine is totally present in each one. And, of course, it is mirrored interestingly in the human body. Many today are interested in reflexology. The whole system of the organism, the body, is reflected in the sole of the foot and in the palm of the hand, and also in the eyes (iridology). Nature's method is everywhere, putting the whole into all the parts. Each part represents — makes present — the whole. That leads us to the understanding of the human being as a microcosm, a little world. The whole universe is present in each one of us. We are a little world in ourselves, and the whole world is mirrored in each particular part. This is the view which is gradually coming through to me. It is so wonderful.

It is reflected in all the great religious traditions. Hinduism has the *advaita* of Shankara. Today — and this is rather important — we are recognizing that Shankara did not say the world is illusory. He said neither *sat* nor *asat,* neither "being" nor "not being." It is something between the two, and it has relative being — it has no being in itself. In that sense the universe is pure illusion, but it has being in relation to the Divine, to the Brahman. Interestingly, Saint Thomas

Aquinas, they say, has exactly the same understanding: that the created universe has being in relation to God. It has no being in itself. Besides Shankara and Saint Thomas Aquinas, there is Gotama, who was the great authority for Mahayana Buddhism, and even the Universal Man (*al-insan al Kamil*) in the Sufi tradition. All three had the same understanding. So we can safely say that this is the universal wisdom. I think this is what we are coming to today; and it is so important, because behind all the differences of religion — which are infinite on the scale of multiplicity — and when we get beyond all the multiplicity to unity, we find a common tradition, a common wisdom that we all share. That is the hope for the future: that religions will discover their own depth. As long as they remain on their surface, they will always be divided in conflict. When they discover their depth, then we converge on the unity.

As an illustration, I sometimes use the fingers and the palm of the hand. Each finger represents a religion. The baby finger is Buddhism, the next is Hinduism, the middle one is Islam, the forefinger is Judaism, and the thumb is Christianity. Buddhism is miles from Christianity. And they are all divided separately, but as you go deep into any religion, you converge on the center, and everything springs from that center and converges at that center, which is how we are today.

❖

When I thought I was going to die after the stroke, it came through to me that one has to be ready to die — at every moment, really, certainly every day. I think this is a lesson

94

for everybody. Nobody knows when he is going to die. It is no good simply putting it off all the time, as we tend to do. If you face it, you realize you hold your life in your hands, and you're ready to let go at any moment. I think that is real wisdom.

In fact, it was Plato who said that human existence is preparing to die, and this is deeply true. Of course, we mustn't forget this is the meaning of resurrection. Resurrection is, precisely, going through death.

One thing that came through to me in that stroke experience was the death of Christ. We hear "My God, My God, why have you forsaken me?" Jesus was dying on the cross and he had been rejected by his people. He had been persecuted by the Roman government. He was physically in pain and psychologically in distress, and he had to face the darkness of death. He had to go through the total darkness. He had to lose his God, in a sense. Any god is a projection, and eventually we have to get rid of all projections. The mind has to go; then, beyond the mind, we enter into the darkness, which is the darkness of love.

Saint Gregory of Nyssa said that beyond the purgative is the illuminative way, the way of light; and beyond that is the unitive way, the way of love in the darkness. So Jesus went through the darkness into total love. At that moment he became total love because he surrendered everything. Body and soul have been totally surrendered in love. Then he is taken up in the life of the Spirit.

We should not forget that the appearances to the disciples were just appearances. They were not the Resurrection, as some people imagine. Lots of people have appeared after their death, actually. Jesus' appearances were more dramatic, and they had a more deep significance, but they were only appearances. Jesus was preparing the disciples for the moment when he would go beyond. That is where he is now. He has gone beyond. This is, perhaps, an interesting insight into the Eucharist, because many people, I think, misunderstand the Eucharist. They think that Jesus is present there in some sort of bodily form. But the reality is that the bread and the wine signify and represent — make present — the whole mystery of Christ. That includes his body and blood which were offered on the cross, but it's now the body and blood of the Resurrection. It is not the body on the cross, which is gone forever.

I learned my sacramental theology from the works of Saint Thomas Aquinas. He makes a very clear distinction between the *sacramentum et res*. The sacramental is the sign, the bread and the wine are the sacramental, but the thing signified is the *res,* the reality. Aquinas said that the bread and the wine are the sign, the outward sign, the visible sign. They signify, first of all, the body and blood of Christ. But then again, the body and blood of Christ are signs of the total reality of Christ. So under the sign of the bread and the wine is Jesus in his self-manifestation on earth. In his flesh and his blood his sacrifice on the cross is present, but taken up into the totality of the divine life. The entire reality is present under these signs. The body and blood in the Eucharist are the body and blood of the Resurrection that is not in time and space.

Saint Thomas Aquinas is very clear that Jesus is not just in time and space. He is present in time and space, as well as beyond time and space. That is why he can be present in every altar on the earth, but in his spiritual body, which is beyond the physical. He is one with God, and that is the spiritual body. The whole universe is present in that spiritual body.

What we encounter in the Eucharist is not simply Jesus dying and rising again, although that is basic to it. We encounter Jesus in his transcendent state in the Resurrection. He is one with the Father. The whole mystical body of Christ is present. Saint Augustine puts it beautifully when he says that the bread that you place on the altar is yourself you are placing on the altar. We offer ourselves under the signs of bread and wine, and we become the mystical body of Christ. We are taken into the whole mystery. The mystery is wonderful, but many people stop at the outer appearance of it, which is a great difficulty.

This process of change since my stroke has been very gradual. It is going on all the time. It is not easy to put into words, but something is happening all the time. It is partly a physical transformation. The body itself is undergoing great changes. My problem before was that I was living largely from the head; and then after the stroke, I got down into the heart. But now it goes right from the heart to all the *chakras*,* right to the root *chakra*. The root *chakra* is the body's connection to the earth. What I feel now is that the spirit is coming down. I always think the *sahasrara*† is above the body, and it descends to the head. Then it goes down from the head through the throat to the heart. And now it is descending to the belly, which is very impor-

---

* "Energy wheels," a series of energy centers that run along the spinal column of the body, as defined in Kundalini Yoga, which is a division of Tantric Yoga.
† The crown or coronal *chakra*. It is located on the top of the head and is related to the experience of self-realization or enlightenment.

tant. The *hara** — that is where all the blood is — is in the belly. It is your flesh and your blood that this has to penetrate. It then moves down through the sex region. That is very important, too, because that tends to be suppressed. In my own experience it was very much repressed. I am rediscovering the whole sexual dimension of life at the age of eighty-six, really. And that also means discovering the feminine. So the whole of this dimension, which I had been seeking for a very long time, is now sort of opening itself up to me.

I think the Mother is gradually revealing itself to me and taking over. But it is not the Mother alone. It is the Mother and the Father, the male and the female, sort of gradually having their marriage. The whole thing is becoming integrated, but it's a continual process. I can't say that it is fully realized. In fact, it is certainly not fully realized. This integration is taking place all the time, and it is quite bewildering at times. There are always the opposite forces working, but something is happening all the time — a sort of inner transformation.

Sometimes, I get in a state of bewilderment and confusion, and then I meditate. I let it all sort itself out. I don't try to sort it out, but I enter into silence, into emptiness, and allow all this confusion, these things, to settle. Then the order comes out of the chaos, again and again. You let the order come out of the chaos. Don't try to arrange it. The danger is, of course, to get it under control, because then it does not work. This is a temptation all the time for me.

It is very difficult to explain, because it's not fully formed

---

*In some yogic systems, the power center or third chakra is referred to as the *hara,* and it relates to raw emotions, power drives, and social identification.

in my mind; it does not come into the rational consciousness properly. It is always just beyond. I think the best way I can explain it is that the rational consciousness is dividing and separating all the time, and the distinctions remain when the separation disappears. So you don't confuse things.

I like to use the illustration of the symphony. Mozart could apparently conceive a total symphony in one note. But it does not mean the notes are confused. It means every single note and passage and harmony is there, but it is all contained in a moment. The whole is specifically contained in that moment. It is an awareness that all the differences are there. We should be able to relate to people and situations as they come, but each encounter is contained in a wider unity, a deeper unity, as part of an ongoing process. We can't properly put it into words. It is always going beyond words, beyond the rational mind. It is like a horizon, in a sense. We are on a journey and come upon the horizon; and it is embracing everything, and everything is contained in it. But still we are in search, in a sense, of the fullness beyond the horizon.

When my rational mind is bewildered, I begin to discover. This is another very interesting thing. I find that my body knows much more than my mind; and when I have to do something, the body does it before the mind does. Now, if I have to get up and walk somewhere, the body will get up and walk out, and then the mind will agree: "Oh, yes, that's what I wanted to do." But it is really the body that works first. This is most interesting. It means, of course, that we have a mental faculty that is based in the brain, but we also have an intuitive awareness, more like an animal's in a way, which knows what to do in any situation; and that mind gradually takes over. Then, of course, we have to harmonize the two. Sometimes the rational mind objects to what the body wants to do, but normally the body always knows much better than the rational mind does.

It means that the body has opened itself up, not to the rational mind, but to the deeper mind beyond. It has really been guided from the Spirit within. Slowly, the Spirit is taking over both the mind and the body and is penetrating the whole, and integrating the whole. But it is a slow process.

❖

The chaos is in God. Creation is chaos. From out of the depths of the Divine Mystery, the whole of creation comes forth, and it's not simply the intelligible world, as Plato and others would have thought. God is not simply in the light, in the intelligible world, in the rational order. God is in the darkness, in the womb, in the Mother, in the chaos from which the order comes. So the chaos is in God, we could say, and that is why discovering the darkness is so important. We tend to reject it as evil and as negative and so on, but the darkness is the womb of life. Yet we are always trying to discover how to relate the opposites. You cannot dismiss one or the other. You have to be open to the *coincidencia oppositorum,* the coincidence of opposites. That is the secret.

There is always order in chaos. And the more one discovers the order — the *rita,* the rhythm of the universe — the more one discovers that it is the chaos which is behind it all. And so we try to bring the chaos and the order together. This does not mean eliminating the chaos. We see this in the movement in science today. Behind all the order is chaotic movement that cannot be described or visualized or even mathematically examined. It is something really beyond the human mind, and yet the whole order of the universe is coming out of that chaos. I think that enlightenment is the union of this divine reality with the chaos of life, of nature, of matter, of the world. One is trying always to relate to the physical universe and all the confusions of life. The two are not something to be dismissed, but are integral to the whole state of understanding.

When reflecting back over my stroke, though it is not easy to recall in detail, I focus on one or two aspects: first, this sense of total darkness, facing the darkness, the annihilation in a way, the total emptiness. As it is something a person has to go through, as I did, he must not reject it. One has to simply accept it, totally. Jesus on the cross was my model there. I felt convinced that he went through this stage of total death, of annihilation. He let go of everything, and only then could he, as a human being, become total love.

I recall another aspect. When I woke up at night and I thought I was going to die, I felt the coming of Christ. I recall one great friend of mine telling me of a friend of hers who was dying and who asked her if he was coming. That was my question, too: "Is he coming?" I felt the coming of Christ. So that if I were to die, it would simply be entering into that presence. That was how it was for me.

❖

When I came back from Europe on this last trip, I thought I would be in Shantivanam. It would now be very peace-

101

ful, and everything would come together; but there has been more chaos. I begin to realize that the deeper one goes, the more one has to become aware of the opposites, the chaos, and the darkness. This does not mean running away from the chaos, but letting it come more and more into your life, to integrate more and more elements in your life.

I told many people I was not going to travel anymore, and I had retired to this hermitage. I would be alone and I would meditate and I would be by myself. Then, quite unexpectedly, I got drawn out of it. People invited me. I felt the call and the need. I think America was the first.

There is a great deal of American culture that I don't like, but I found a tremendous vitality, especially in California, far more than in India. In India the tradition is there, but people are not inquiring in the same way. In California they are investigating everything: every aspect of psychology, philosophy, religion, and whatever — even drugs, etc. There is much chaos, again, but tremendous new growth is also taking place. I began to see, more and more, that the world today is in this state of chaos and America is a chaos, out of which a new order is emerging. When I went to Australia, I found it even more there. Australia is a younger country and, I think, more open in some ways.

This experience grows daily, but it has its ups and downs. There are times of confusion, times of darkness, but there is a continual growth. It's quite extraordinary, because, I think, in the last two years I have grown more than in the previous eighty-four years. The growth process is very interesting. It gets more intense as you go on. It is continuous, and that's why it is difficult to put it into words. I don't even know exactly what is happening. Very often it is so profound, with changes taking place all the time.

8

Science and Religion

M Y INTEREST in science developed only in the last ten years at most, when I attended a congress, or meeting, in Bombay of scientists and psychologists and spiritual leaders. Mother Teresa was there. The Dalai Lama had been invited, but I think he was not able to come. It was there I discovered the new movement in physics and the new movement in psychology. I didn't actually "discover" it; rather, I had been learning about it, and I found it all coming together there. And I've completely changed my attitude to science.

Until recently, we applied Newtonian science, with its really mechanistic view of the universe; this was the scientific orthodoxy. As I understood it, the Newtonian view was that the universe consists of solid bodies moving in space and time. When we get down to the atom, and divide the atom...well, it could not be split. So there were these solid bodies that were moving about and making up the whole material world. Then the physicists actually split the atom, and they discovered the particles again that make up the atom: electrons and protons, and so on. Then another breakthrough came in the 1920s, with the discovery that you cannot eventually limit the subatomic world to particles. The particles dissolve into waves, and this was a terrible experience for Niels Bohr and his companion, Heisenberg, in Denmark. It's as if the whole basis of their science seemed to be collapsing, but they faced it out. It is now believed that the universe is a field of energies, these energies working at different frequencies and structured in such a way that we perceive them as matter.

I think what strikes me more than anything else, partly on this view of nonduality, is the conflict of opposites: that the universe is composed of a conflict of opposites at every level, and we are now going through a period of tremendous conflict. The universe is really falling apart, I think. Politically, socially, economically, and, above all, religiously, I think we are going through a period of disintegration.

Always, in nature, disintegration is the moment of rebirth. As you disintegrate, you lose your center. You recover a new center, and something new emerges. In fact, I am told, in evolution an organism has a center, and it organizes all its elements around that center. But at the same time, it is always being affected by the environment. It is pulling you out in this direction and that direction. If the pull of the environment becomes too great, that center loses its place, and a new center has to be found; then a new organism comes into being. So, I think the present systems of politics and economics and religion are organized around a certain center that has been valid for many years and is now breaking down. The pull of the world around us is one of disintegration. The whole of the system is breaking down. A new center has to be found, and is being found, I think, all over the world. People are discovering a deeper center of reality in their own lives. This is working itself out in the universe.

I think we have got to face up to the fact: We are entering a period of tremendous conflict and disintegration, disillusion and rebirth. It is actually taking place now, individually and socially, and is going to change the whole course of human history. How it will take shape no one knows.

This reminds me of a poem by Yeats in which he said all things fall apart. He saw it. From the chaos a new center emerges, and then it begins to reintegrate all the different aspects of life in a new paradigm, a new understanding. The New Age is emerging, but with tremendous conflict. We have got to go through the suffering and the pain and the crucifixion, if you like. But the rebirth is there, and is taking place, and will create a new world. None of us can see what form it will take, but we have faith and confidence that it is coming into being.

It is only through the human being that the universe breaks through now into a new reality. We hear so much talk of "the kingdom of God is at hand." The whole message of the gospel is that something is going to happen. I think change is always occurring, in a sense, but now is particularly the moment when this dramatic change is going to take place.

Science today sees the universe as a field of energies with the energies moving at different frequencies, which creates the appearance of a three-dimensional world. We really project this through our senses and our minds. Scientists see it as an analogy of a hologram, where you take a photo and you just see the vibrations of light; and then you put a stronger laser beam through it, and within the hologram the three-dimensional form emerges and it's in every part of it. So Western science now sees the universe as this field of energies and structure in the same way. I read one book that changed my mind, actually. I think it was before I went to the congress in Bombay. It was *The Tao of Physics* by Fritjof Capra, an Austrian physicist. He described this new movement in science and related it to the Eastern traditions to which it bore an extraordinarily close resemblance, particularly the Buddhist and the Taoist — the difference being that the Western world still thinks of that field of energy simply as energy. Westerners cannot really place consciousness, or the mind, in relation to it. The Eastern world has always seen it as a field of energies that is integrated in consciousness. People in the East see the whole universe as energy structured by consciousness and coming out of a center that is beyond the energy and the consciousness and is the source of all. That is very near to the Christian idea of the Trinity. The Holy Spirit is that energy which penetrates the whole universe. That energy is organized by the Word, the wisdom that comes forth from the beginning. Both the energy and the Word come from the primordial mystery that transcends everything. That, I think, is the view of the universe today.

And this new thinking is not limited to physics. Biologist Rupert Sheldrake came to this ashram [Saccidananda] and wrote his first book, *The New Science of Life*, while staying here. He is at the same point of advancement in biology as the others are in physics. He believes that you cannot explain organic life in terms of mechanism, as physicists try to do. You have to understand the whole biological world as an organic whole, see it as interrelated, and the answer comes through everywhere. The universe is, as Fritjof Capra called it, "a complicated web of interdependent relationships." You cannot explain it in any other terms, and that, of course, is exactly how the universe is conceived, particularly in the Mahayana tradition. The universe is this cosmic whole, in which the unity is manifested in all the multiplicity of interrelated elements. So the whole universe is a web of interrelated, interdependent relationships, all parts of a cosmic whole; and that is our vision of the world today.

This leads us to the understanding of nonduality. Nonduality is essentially the understanding of relationship. The ordinary, rational, logical mind divides, analyzes, separates. That is one way, and it is an important way of understanding things; but it is extremely limited. The deeper mind, the intuitive mind, whatever you like to call it, goes beyond all these separate things and perceives the whole as manifested in the part. You cannot understand the parts except in relation to the whole. Exactly the same applies in the spiritual world. We have this tremendous division between good and evil, light and darkness, truth and error, God and the world — that is our systematic understanding of the universe. I feel, as with Newtonian physics, that such an understanding really belongs to the past. It is perfectly valid on its own level, just as Newtonian physics is a marvelous achievement and explains the universe, at one level, extremely effectively. But it breaks down at a certain point. So this dualistic view of God and the world, of good and evil, and so on does explain the world at a certain level of understanding, but it is a limited level. It is producing terrible results today, and terribly negative effects. We are challenged today, just as in science, to go beyond that religious paradigm and discover the nondual reality.

As I've said before, the key to that is the Christian doctrine of the Trinity. It is extremely interesting that most people, Christians as well as Jews and Moslems, think of God as a monad — one being, one person, a personal God who is organizing the universe. Though that is useful and helpful in many ways, it is only a projection of the mind. Beyond that personal god in every religious tradition, we understand there is a transcendent mystery that probably has no name. It comes out very clearly, of course, in the Hindu tradition. There are the gods and goddesses, of course, but also Brahman. He is the unity beyond all dualities. In Buddhism it is exactly the same. There is *nirvana* or *sunyata:* the void. And all the multiplicity of nature is contained within that unity beyond the mind. Islam is very interesting. There is Allah, the supreme personal god, judging everybody and bringing condemnation right and left. The Sufi mystics go beyond the personal god to Allah, the reality. They speak of that reality in nondual terms. As the whole universe is a web of interdependent relationship, so the godhead, the ultimate reality, as far as we can conceive it, is a communion of being in relationship. The Trinity, as mentioned before, is being in relationship, being known in consciousness as the Word, as distinct from its source, and communicating in the Spirit, in the energy that flows from the Word, the wisdom.

We are beginning to see that this nondual relationship is the basis for the whole universe expressing itself in the Word, in the intellect, in the mind. The mind communicates itself, giving itself to the world, to the energy that flows from it. So the Trinity really is the nearest we could come in human understanding to the original structure of the universe and the source of the universe.

I feel there is a complete convergence now of science and

111

religion; scientists in the West have arrived where the Eastern mystic already is and where the Christian mystic also can arrive. In his wonderful book, *The Unity of Reality*, my friend Michael von Brooke studies this whole concept of nonduality, and Shankara and the Indian tradition. He touches also on the Buddhist tradition and shows how the Christian doctrine of the Trinity is the most adequate expression of the mystery of nonduality. The Father, the Son, and the Spirit are not three, and they are not one. They are interrelated beings, being in relationship, which is communion in love. Love is relationship. And if God is love, then there must be relationship in God. If God is simply a monad, then he cannot really be called love.

9

Seasoned Thoughts

Opening to the Sacred

I THINK FROM HINDUISM, above all, I learned the sense of the sacred. I'd been searching for it, but the Western world is profane: We have deliberately eliminated every sign of the sacred, except in some churches and particular places. In India there are holy temples and places, but the earth itself is sacred, as well as the air and the water and the fire. You are living in a sacred world there. It's particularly true in the villages. In the towns they begin to lose it.

I also discovered the sacred expressing itself in language and the *Upanishads*. They take you from this world and the world in which you are living and open you up to the inner dimension of life. Behind all the outer phenomena is the Brahman, the reality. You learn to see through the outer world to the inner reality, and then you take your own body and outer self and you learn to discover the inner self, the Atman, the spirit within. So your whole being opens up to another dimension — a fourth dimension — beyond the body, the senses, and the mind; and you discover the transcendent mystery which embraces the universe. It is in your

114

depths, in the depths of your own heart. That, I think, is what Hinduism has to give.

The Cosmic Christ

Reflecting back on Christianity, I began to discover its cosmic dimension, which we have so much lost. We focus on the human Christ, or the divine person, and we forget the whole cosmic dimension which was very strong in the early Church. It is basic, really, but is so easily lost. We need to see the cosmic Christ. Saint Paul said: " . . . in Him, and through Him, and for Him, all things were created, and in Him all things hold together." The universe holds together in Christ. We can begin to see that the Hindu vision of the sacred universe, in our understanding, is made sacred by the presence of Christ. It is not only sacred by creation's sake, but by redemption, because sin has entered into the world — evil, conflict, violence, destruction, and death. The world had to be redeemed from all the negative forces; and redemption is dying to this. Jesus died to the whole creation, the whole world of sin and suffering and death, and opened it up to resurrection, to new life. The whole of cosmos and the whole of humanity is taken up into the new life because Jesus died for all humanity — not for Jews or Christians or any particular people, but the whole of humanity.

Through creation, humanity is redeemed and opened up to the transcendent mystery, which is Brahman, which is Atman, which is Tao, which is *nirvana*. These are different names for what cannot be expressed. Everything we can say about God and the Infinite is limited, is symbolic, is a type of analogy, and points to something that cannot be

115

expressed. Every religion points toward this inexpressible mystery. That's the only way we can get beyond our conflicts. If we remain in our own religious conditions, with different languages, different modes of thought, expression, and so on, we are all in conflict. We kill one another in defending our particular beliefs. When we go beyond the images, the concepts, the sacramental aspect, the signs, to the reality, then we discover unity that embraces the whole creation, all humanity, and all religion. So that's what we are really seeking today, I think. And it's coming, but slowly and in spite of all the conflicts that arise.

The Catholic Church

My first thoughts of entering the Church came when I was reading the New Testament. This quite changed my mind. First of all was the realization that Jesus himself never said he was God. Some people imagine he did, but he spoke of having a unique relationship to God. "No one knows the Son but the Father, no one knows the Father but the Son," and that unique relationship he came to share with his disciples. He formed a group of disciples around him. He chose twelve of them to be apostles, to spread the message. They formed a community. Before he died, he gathered his little community together and celebrated this meal with them, which was really his giving his life for the world in that community.

And so, the Church is the community that grew out of Jesus' union with his disciples and his giving his life for his disciples. This came naturally to me, once I really accepted

116

Christ as having this unique relationship with God. I *had* to accept the community that shares that relationship.

I think we have to face the fact that the Church is a movement in history: It is affected by all the social and historical conditions of the time. The Church often gets fixed in a particular mode of thought and expression and goes on with that even when it ceases to be relevant. We have undergone tremendous social and psychological changes recently. In many ways the Church has not kept up with them. It keeps using the old language and old methods that no longer work.

I think the most serious thing is the very negative attitude to the body, to sex, to nature. Children are brought up with this negative attitude toward their body, their senses, their feelings, and get a bad image of themselves — they are guilty, they are sinners — and this is terribly destructive. In the past it seemed to work. People were very tough, and the more you hit them down, the more they came up; but today people are very vulnerable, and the old method simply is destructive.

It is a question of the way we present the gospel. If we present it in a certain language and in a certain tradition of thought, it becomes absolutely destructive, instead of being creative. We have not yet learned the lesson, I am afraid.

Matthew Fox, with his *Creation Spirituality, Original Blessing,* and other books, has tried to counter that. And I think he is right, in a sense. I think there is a place for sin — I am sure for redemption — in the Church, but it has to be placed in context. The context is the human being created in the image of God. We all have this divine presence within us and when we realize that, sin can become meaningful. But

117

when we don't have that context or framework, and we're told we are sinful and evil — that is, simply, destructive. It produces a totally negative effect that, I think, more than anything else, puts people off the Church.

Unfortunately, we still have the old tradition. When we start the mass, for example, we say "[As we] prepare ourselves to celebrate this sacred mystery, let us call to mind our sins." That is probably the last thing that people want to do at the moment. We should call to mind the love of God, the grace that has brought us together, the love that is uniting us. Then we can talk about sin after that. We realize we fail in love, of course, but to put it first is terribly misleading. That is our main problem.

Moving Beyond the Self

For me, sin is self-centeredness. We have fallen from a state where we are centered in God, in truth, and in love. We fall into the ego, and the ego is the principle of the whole psyche. The soul is centered on an ego, a separate personality. In a sense the ego is good: We need a separate personality. The child has to separate from the mother and become a person. But then, if one is to get beyond his limited person, he has to be open to others — and eventually open to God.

But we get stuck in our ego, our separate personality. We are self-centered, full of self-love and self-obsession. Our whole world centers around "me." And if everyone else is doing the same thing, we are in conflict with one another. We create a world of separate selves, all in conflict, instead of realizing the important difference between the individual and the person. The individual is separate. We have a unique

118

body, a unique soul; but in the depth of our being, what we call the spirit, we are interrelated, we are one with others. If we don't discover that, then we live in this separated self and become a center of conflict and violence in the end. That's the tragedy.

Despair comes from the ego. We are centered on our ego; and when the ego is getting all that it wants, we feel very happy. When it is frustrated, we feel complete despair, and it's a sign or challenge to get out of our ego. In each of us there is a deeper self, where we are totally free from depression — if we will open our mind and our heart, mainly in meditation. This is how we learn to observe ourself — our feelings, feelings of depression and despair, and then detach from those feelings. Then awareness of the deeper self emerges. Then our whole situation can change in a moment. It is a way of breaking out of our ego, and opening up to the real self and to the meaning of life. It is a challenge when one is in despair.

The meaning of life lies precisely in realizing that we are imprisoned in our ego, in the limited human self; and within us, and beyond us, are infinite beauty and truth and love. We can discover that, once we have let go of our ego, our limited self. There are two ways to do this: One is through meditation, which I think is the most direct; the other is to fall in love. The challenge is to get out of yourself. Love takes you out of your self, and if you can fall in love with somebody, or with God, or something beyond you, that could take you out of the ego. Unless you can get out of your ego, there is no answer to life.

When AIDS, or cancer, or any disease, comes and threatens your life, you are challenged to go beyond the limited self, to realize that there is this reality of truth and love. It is in you and around you. Once you let go of the ego, the self, everything can open up. AIDS, cancer, a breakdown — any of these things — can be transcended at the moment we are challenged to open up and discover the real meaning of our life. There is no doubt: It can be a grace.

Many believe that the Catholic Church has been one of the most uncompassionate organizations known to man, that it has condoned, or aligned itself with, some of greatest atrocities and cruelties in human history. I think the first thing is to recognize that this is true. We cannot deny that the Inquisition was one of the worst horrors in history. Hitler and Stalin were just on the same line, really. It went on for centuries, and it was brought to India by Saint Francis Xavier. That is a reality.

There were the crusades against the Moslems and, worst of all perhaps, the crusades against the Albigensians, who were considered heretics. It was simply a massacre. And the way that the Spaniards and Portuguese massacred the native people of the Americas is appalling. There were also the wars of religion, which went on for ages, and the persecution of heretics that goes on today. It does no good trying to hide these things. With all this going on, it is easy to get the impression of a total lack of compassion.

The thirteenth century was the great age of the culture of the Church. We had the great theologians like Saint Thomas Aquinas, all the great cathedrals, all the marvels of art and poetry and Dante, all the great mystics. Yet at the same time, the Inquisition was just getting into force. So we have to face this. Life is like this. We want to think some things are good and some are bad, some light and some dark. But the reality is that light and dark, good and evil, are always interwoven. We need to be able to discern. If we face the evil in the Church and the reality of it — in the present day as well as in the past — we can also recognize there is an extraordinary light and truth and goodness, which never fails. The only reason I am a Catholic is because I believe, and have discovered, that within the Church is this truth, this love, this grace, this compassion, this goodness, which is the meaning of life. But I cannot deny that the opposite is there also. If we try to deny it, we have a false picture of the Church.

Transforming Consciousness

Unfortunately, the fear of God is considered the beginning of wisdom. Wisdom is the fear of God, but a fear with two meanings. One is a sense of awe, of reverence — and that is what the theological fear really is. That is acceptable; but for most people it means the contrary: a sense of one's own inadequacy. There are forces contrary to us that we cannot face, and these are negative and destructive. They do have a deeper, positive meaning, but people have lost sight of that. They see only the negative sense — again and again — because their language is wrong. It is no longer relevant, and that's my point.

As long as we think that the rational mind can understand the universe and God, we are precisely in this state of illusion. Every spiritual tradition realizes we have to get beyond our rational mind and logical thought and open up to a deeper level of consciousness. When we do that, we

121

get another perspective. As long as our God is a god of the rational consciousness and we expect him to behave as he ought to behave, then we have no place for God. We just have to get rid of this notion. Once we understand that God is the mystery in which we are all involved, the mystery of existence, our reason can shed some light on it. But far beyond the reason, there is the intuitive instinct: an intuitive power in the mind, which is actually the power of love. It is love knowledge, and when we discover that, we begin to see that we cannot explain rationally all the suffering and the tragedy of the world.

There are different ways of approaching transformation. For many people, I always say meditation is the way. They have to learn to sit quietly, and calm their body and their mind and then keep open to their inner self. We have to see beyond our body, beyond our mind. If one sits quietly he can discover that there is a deeper self, a deeper awareness. Some people find it simply looking around at nature — the trees, the birds, the sea, the river, or whatever. The key is to discover something beyond our body and beyond our ordinary rational, conventional mind, to discover that deep self, which then can grow. Take the example of a seed: It is waiting all the time. Once we discover that, we can grow and our life can be transformed. The reason why many people do not believe in God, or anything, is because they are totally centered in their ego, this limited human separated self. The challenge is to get out of that. Whether we call it God or not is not very important. We can discover that there is something beyond ourself, beyond this present world as we understand it, where the real meaning of life is found.

Celibacy

I have a very special view on celibacy. In the early church, first of all, there were no priests. By the end of the first century priesthood began to be established. The priests were normally married, just like the apostles. We know Peter was married, and the other apostles probably were, too. Jesus served married men. The early priests and elders who were called were married people. Then, in the third and fourth century, a movement grew up in the Church to embrace monastic life. The monk was to be celibate. He gave up family, friends, home, everything, to follow Christ — and that is a particular calling.

Monastic life is perfectly distinct from the priesthood. The monks were not priests. It was said there are two people whom monks should avoid at all cost: women and bishops. Women will try to get you married, and bishops will try to make you a priest. Unfortunately, from the fourth century onward, the monks were seen as rather model Christians. So the tendency grew for monks to become celibate and monks to become priests, and the two vocations have never been separated. Today we need to separate the vocations. In the Orthodox Church priests are married. I think we should go back to a married priesthood and recognize celibacy is a particular gift given to some people. If one has a gift for service to the people in a parish, he doesn't necessarily have a gift for celibacy. On the other hand, a person with a gift for celibacy may have no call whatever to serve people in the parish. So we should keep the two vocations distinct. They are complementary, each necessary for the Church, but they should not be mixed up. Which is what has really happened today.

The Church and the Feminine

The status of women in the Church is also a big problem, which goes right back to the Old Testament. We must realize the Old Testament came from a patriarchal culture. There was a matriarchal culture in the surrounding people in Canaan and Egypt and Babylon and so on. Israel reacted against the whole of that matriarchal culture — the Mother Goddess, the fertility of the earth, and the feminine. It was a necessary movement, for the transcendent God is beyond all nature, beyond the feminine, the passive, the human, the earthy. God is utterly transcendent. But they put down the feminine aspect, the nature, and life and, above all, the sexuality. I think it was a necessary stage. We have to transcend nature and life, transcend the feminine, just as the child has to leave the mother and go out and become a man. But we have gone out beyond the feminine, rejected the feminine, sex, earth, matter, and life, to build up this wonderful religion of grace and truth and so on. Now I think we have to reconcile. We have to recover the balance.

Today we recognize that the Church, as it has been organized in Europe and throughout the world, belongs to a patriarchal culture. Our names for God are all masculine, and the Apostles were all masculine, and the bishops are all masculine. All things have their time, and this patriarchal system was valid in its time. But it is no longer valid.

Today we are discovering the values of the feminine in normal human life everywhere, and slowly we are discovering them in the Church. We shall eventually discover them in God. God is feminine as well as masculine. There is no point in making God one and not the other. So I think we are in a

124

moment of awakening — discovering, really. We see the imbalance of our whole cultural tradition. We have to change that and rediscover the feminine in the Church, in life, in human nature, and in the whole of the cosmos. This is the movement of the present day. All that has been neglected is gradually coming back. And that's the hope of the future.

Expressing the Faith

I think the way the faith is presented in the Church is often quite irrelevant, and that's why you see ninety percent of the people in Europe are leaving the Church today. Not because they don't want a religion, or faith, or even Christ, but because they cannot accept the way it's presented to them. The doctrinal system, the liturgical system, the whole moral system, above all. The whole setting of the Church doctrine today belongs to a past age. It is no longer relevant.

Take the way the mystery of Christ is presented, for instance. We are discovering how to present it, but it is a very slow process. There is a conservative force that is afraid of giving up the past. If they give that up, they worry, then everything may go. So they dare not change the language, the concepts, the mode of presentation.

Pope John XXIII, who was a really holy man, made a very important statement. He said, "The substance of the faith remains the same, but the mode of its expression changes.... " It has to change according to the changing environment of human nature and human society. Today we have to present the gospel in a new way, in a language which is relevant to people and to the world around us. We cannot go on presenting it in the language of the past. For example, in India all the missionaries came as Europeans, and naturally they established a European way of life. In the mass they put on European vestments, and they had candles and altars all in European style. This was quite relevant at one time, but it is totally irrelevant here. It is not the culture of India, at all.

It is simply a matter of the way of the cultural tradition in which the faith is presented. If we cling to the past, we simply become irrelevant. If we have the courage to change, then the message comes through in a way which is meaningful to people. That is the hope.

Life is a paradox, and the good and the evil, the black and the white, are always mixed. If you look at the black alone, you get an appalling picture. If you look at the light alone, you get an illusory picture also. The reality is that the Church has all this dark side, this shadow, as well as this incredible light. And what is so bewildering, in a sense, is that the light and the darkness go together.

Writing

From the time I was about sixteen, writing became the ambition of my life. I could not write poetry, but I had a passion for prose. Walter Pater was my model in many ways. Also, Gustave Flaubert, who with his doctrine of the *"mot juste"* could always find just the right word. I cultivated this desire to try to write prose that would be perfectly expressive of the mind with pure truth and reality. The opening pages of my first book, *The Golden String,* are the model of what I was aiming at all that time. I have very rarely achieved it, but it remained an ideal for many years. When I became a monk, I rather lost that ideal. I think I was more interested

in theology, and certainly poetry, especially criticism of poetry. Eventually, I was asked to write articles and reviews,
and then books.

When I was at Pluscarden Priory in Scotland, I was set
free. As novice master there, I had very few duties. I was
free to write, and a friend of mine suggested I write up my
story. I sat down every day after breakfast for about two
hours and began to write. It just came out, just flowed out. I
forget how long it took — maybe six months. That was my
first experiment in writing a full-length piece.

When I first came to India, I didn't write, but I did some
translations. When I came here to Shantivanam, I began
to write *Return to the Center*. It is very interesting, looking
back now, that this book came out absolutely spontaneously.
I wrote it in longhand completely, and made no corrections
at all. It just came out like that. It's extraordinary. I think
The Marriage of East and West was probably the same. I
continued to write several works exploring the relationship
between Christianity and the religions of the East.

I used to type at one time but was not much good at typ-
ing. I simply managed. Eventually, I found it getting more
and more difficult. Now I find it almost impossible to write.
What I do is talk and get somebody to record it. That has
simplified things.

So in a sense I would say writing has ceased to be a major
interest. I just do it when I feel the need. If I have to give a
talk anywhere, I prepare it in my mind; I don't write anything — except perhaps just a few notes sometimes. Writing
was a youthful ambition; but old age has cured me of that
particular desire.

I also published a book called *The New Creation in*

Christ, which was based on the talks I gave in Indiana at the John Main Seminar in 1991. It is about meditation and contemplative life.

I have just prepared a book on the universal wisdom, which consists of readings from the scriptures of the world. I have taken examples of Hinduism, Buddhism, Taoism, Sikhism, Islam, Judaism, and Christianity. I have six short but very fundamental *Upanishads* and the whole of *Bhagavad-Gita,* the whole *Tao te ching,* the Sikh morning and evening prayer, very little from the Koran, but some good extracts from Al Ghazali and Rumi, the Sufi teachers. Then some selections from the Wisdom books only of the Old Testament, and from the gospels, the Sermon on the Mount, the basic story from Mark, the further story with the parables from Luke, and the whole of Saint John's Gospel. In addition, the Letter to the Ephesians, as the sort of gnostic wisdom coming up in the New Testament.

I have written an introduction of about a hundred pages, trying to show how every religion starts from a primitive base in a dualistic style and gradually moves into nondualism. It's very obvious in Hinduism and Buddhism and Taoism, but it is also true in Islam, Judaism, and Christianity. So, to me, the convergence of all religion is in nondualism, which is beyond the rational mind.

Going Beyond

Regarding regrets in my life, there's very little. When I look back, I see there have been tremendous limitations and failures and so on, but all within a limited context, and it's being able to transcend that limited context. When I was in the monastery for twenty-five years, I accepted the whole Church, the whole situation. The whole thing was just the norm for me. I did not feel any discontent with it then; and yet, today, I feel the whole thing was extremely limited. I could not live it again, but that teaches me rather that our lives proceed in stages; and at each stage there is a particular limited horizon, and we have to live within that.

We may have regrets at that stage, and we may have some success and so on. But in any case, neither the regrets nor the successes are of ultimate significance. It is always being able to move beyond your limited stages, and to keep open to the transcendent.

When we look back on the whole of our life, we see it as a mixture — good and evil, failure and success — but we realize that that is not the real thing. Something must move within us, through it all, taking us beyond it all.

I was once told the story about a fisherman in Kerala who was lying on the beach when a well-meaning Westerner came up and said, "Why do you lie here doing nothing? You should be out fishing. I can help you to get a boat, and to get an engine for the boat and I can provide nets for you and you can go out to the deeper water and get a good catch and then make money, and then you'll be able to get a nice house and have a very nice life and do whatever you like." And the man said, "Well, I'm doing what I like now, so I think I prefer to remain where I am."

10

The Reflections of Others

Judy Walter, missionary and close friend of Father Bede:

FATHER BEDE had a stroke on January 25, 1990. I remember that morning well. We were all sitting in the temple waiting for mass to begin. After a few minutes Brother Christudas got up and went to Father's room. I felt an urge to follow him, and so I followed. We found Father Bede lying on the bed, blue. I knew right away that he was seriously ill, but I didn't think what it could be. I just had the feeling that we were losing Father. In that panic, in those few moments, I don't really remember too much of what we did. Except, I remember a doctor was called. Sister Marie Louise, who is a nurse, took charge. She has been taking care of Father all these years.

I remember my feelings at that time were not so much that Father was sick but that Father was leaving us. I felt extreme sadness. I felt that Father was so deep that he was in a place where he couldn't communicate with us anymore,

These are edited transcripts of interviews taken during our filming in December 1992, at Saccidananda Ashram, and afterwards, with those close to Father Bede.

132

and that we may never be able to communicate again. For a few days we lived in that fear that Father was dying. After about three or four days he started to become stronger again.

There was a second experience. On February 25, Father had another death experience. Actually, during the first couple of months he had probably five or six death experiences. The two big ones were January 25 and February 25. On February 25, Father said he was lying in bed, and he felt for sure that Christ was coming for him. He started to say all the prayers of the dying, and he called on our Blessed Mother and all the angels. He said he just lay there waiting, and nothing happened. He realized he was still in the body. Later that day he had this feeling again he was going to die. Now this time he felt that he was being overwhelmed by love. The first time he said it was an experience of the Mother. The destructive. A fearful experience where he felt the blow to the head.

The second time, on February 25, he felt he was being overwhelmed by love. Father was in this experience for over an hour. He was weeping the whole time. Afterward, we were speaking with him, and he started to talk about the experience. "I guess I have to get used to being back in the body again," he said. He explained that somehow, in this feeling of being overwhelmed by love, the Mother had called to him in many different forms. He felt he had the choice either to stay in the body or to leave the body. He said that *he* didn't choose, but something in him chose to remain in the body, and so he remained in the body. It was very difficult for him to go back and to realize that he still had more work to do.

By that time Father was already physically starting to get stronger, and he was taking walks every day, at first with two people supporting him. Then, after a time, he was walking with a cane, and slowly he started to walk by himself. I would say that physically it was only a manifestation of the body growing stronger under the spiritual experience. I think that the body was getting used to the spiritual experience.

Many people noticed that there was a big change in Father. For one thing, I feel that Father is much more warm, open. There is not a reserve there like there was before. He is much more a father. He has always been a father, but now much more. Besides being a spiritual father, he is also a very human father, very warm and loving. I think that many people experienced a real change in that way.

Also, I would say that as far as the things that he says, they come from a different depth. Father doesn't speak of his experience as a stroke. He always speaks of it as his advaitic experience, and I feel that everything he says now, since his *advaitic* experience, is on a totally different level. I remember one night — it was only a few months after he had finished *A New Vision of Reality* — I remember him saying "...when I wrote *A New Vision of Reality* it came from here [pointing to his head]." And he said, "Now since my *advaitic* experience, I feel it's all in here [pointing to his heart]."

Many of us feel that what he says now is coming from a whole different level. Maybe the words are the same. I don't know for sure. Maybe I'm experiencing them differently. Maybe we are all experiencing them differently, but there's definitely been a major change in Father.

Christiane Ropers, M.D.: Ashram guest

I met Father Bede in Germany with my husband, who had worked for him for quite some time. The first time I saw him, I felt real peace, joy, and this very lightness of being, not only in a sense like the sun, but of no heaviness. The body was fully transcendent in a way. You could just lift him up, or he would maybe raise himself.

I had the real privilege of giving him massages. During the massage sessions he would either talk with me, which was just a beautiful experience, or there was silence. I almost preferred the silence, because through the silence there radiates such an intensity from him, but an intensity of peace and quietness. He was not wanting anything, not demanding anything, but just letting himself and the others be. That was a very beautiful experience.

It is wonderful to watch how he has integrated the East, the experience of the East, fully without giving the least of his English personality away. He has remained fully an Englishman — even though he is wearing different clothes, eating differently here, and all that. But his manners, his speech, and, especially, of course, his mentality, I still find totally Western. He is a wonderful example of having integrated the East without losing his Western personality.

Patricia Cave, Australian teacher:

I think I actually met Father Bede in a bookstore in New York. It was about 1986. I was looking for a book by Thomas Merton, and as I took it out of the shelf, a book on the shelf above fell off and literally hit me on the head.

135

I picked it up, and it was titled *Return to the Center.* I was at a period in my life, actually, that was quite a crisis time. I had just discovered meditation in the Christian tradition, a tradition I had left for many years. The title *Return to the Center* spoke to me, so I bought it and I went home to my apartment, and instead of reading the book by Thomas Merton, I read *Return to the Center.*

For the first time, I think, probably in thirty years, somebody spoke on Christianity that I could hear. I heard the words and I could accept them. I remember that period of my life as a period of crisis. I very vividly remember not having slept for about four nights. I went to sleep with that book in my hands, and when I woke up, I finished it. I think I should have known then that he was my teacher, but I didn't, and I never dreamt that I would be here in his presence.

A series of circumstances brought me to India. What Father Bede became to me was a teacher, of course. But I always think of Bede as my healer. He heals by his utter acceptance of not just me, but of everybody. Acceptance of people as they are. I don't know if I had ever actually experienced that before. When I presented him with all my arguments against Christian dogma, he wouldn't argue back. He would say with a twinkle in his eye, "So...well...what can you believe?" By this method he helped me accept many of the things that I couldn't accept before. I think that acceptance came because I felt accepted as a person by him completely. It has always remained that way.

He has taught me the profound truths of life simply by being who he is. For me, Father Bede is humanity. He is the totally integrated human being. He is human. What he has taught me is that the spiritual journey is a journey into total human wholeness. I remember when I first came here, I had no intentions of staying at that time. But I couldn't get over what I thought of as the total integration of masculine and feminine in this man. I had never really seen that before. I think, in the West, we have lost this. This is what I find in India and what I have found in him. And to find somebody whose presence you actually live with who is *so* totally integrated! East and West, I believe, have their meeting point in this man. The masculine and the feminine — he has completely unified the opposites within himself. By doing that, he is a living example that we can all do it, too. I think at this moment this is what he has to bring to the West. Very much so. He is a prophet of our evolution into total humanity.

We can strive after all these experiences — these religious experiences, spiritual experiences — but what it really comes down to is being totally present in our total humanity, and that is what I see in Bede. That is what he gives me all the time. He is completely open to everything. He has opened the scriptures to me. He has opened me to myself. He has sent me up to the Buddhists in the Himalayas, where I now have a Buddhist master. This year he has suggested I go to the Hindu ashrams.

Alison Williams, an English literary editor:

A lot of young Westerners come here, I think, with some trepidation and are quite wary. They come to see what is going on, like myself. It was the first time that I had entered

137

any kind of church for years and years. I stepped inside very gingerly. I think that for a lot of us coming from the West, our experience of spirituality has only been in Christianity, and it's been a very confining, negative, repressive kind of influence on our lives. Even if we're not churchgoers, it has influenced our culture, and I think this is very damaging. So to come here and to hear Father Bede expressing the kinds of things that I am concerned and interested in was amazing. To hear it coming from a Christian, plus a man, plus somebody of a much older generation.

I remember him talking in the first few days I was here about the Bible, on the importance of going beyond the Word. That is something I associate with Father Bede very much. He emphasizes this continuously. He is always talking about going beyond. In almost every talk he gives, he mentions the importance of going beyond.

Father Bede was talking about the Bible and how especially the Old Testament was written at a particular time by particular people. "We have to remember this and focus on the importance of going beyond the Word." They said that the Word was the world. He said it wasn't the world. It only represented the world as they knew it. That is just something I have never heard coming from a Christian before.

He also spoke about the religion of native peoples. He said that aboriginals have known God for forty thousand years. It was beautiful to hear the spirituality of native peoples being recognized, again by a Christian. He also spoke about the importance of the feminine and bringing the feminine back, and ecological issues.

Another thing I like is the way he reminds us, often daily,

138

that we are in India and that so many tragedies are occurring in India — it is not just mystical stuff. He is reminding us of where we are and where this tradition has come from.

Fr. Patrick Eastman, former chaplain at Osage Monastery in Tulsa, Oklahoma, the ashram Father Bede visited while in the United States:

I suppose it is hardly surprising that I have always felt an affinity for Father Bede. Although there is quite a difference in our ages, we were both born in southern England to middle-class Anglican parents. We both had the great fortune to study at Oxford, although Bede's focus was philosophy and literature, while mine was theology.

Bede had the good fortune to be able to sit at the feet of and study with C. S. Lewis, later counting him as a personal friend. C. S. Lewis died just a year or so before I went to St. Stephen's House, the Anglo-Catholic seminary in Oxford, for my studies for the Anglican priesthood. The best I could do in that area was talk with Walter Hooper, Lewis's secretary and companion, who was a frequent visitor to our dining room in St. Stephen's House.

Father Bede, as I am sure you know, was received into full communion with the Roman Catholic Church shortly after his graduation from Oxford and entered the Benedictine Monastery at Prinknash. Again, there was a point of contact for me. Back in the early part of this century, Dom Aelred Carlyle restored the full Benedictine monastic life in the Anglican Church with a monastery on Caldy Island off the South Coast of Wales. In the early 1920s Dom Aelred and most of the community joined the Roman Catholic Church, establishing their monastery at Prinknash. Those who remained within the Church of England eventually came to Nashdom Abbey, and I was associated with that community as a Benedictine oblate.

If these links seem rather tenuous to you, they certainly were points of affinity that I felt with Father Bede. However, after those points of contact, Father Bede's life soars away to far greater distinction. Reading Bede's own autobiography, *The Golden String,* I was made very aware of what a special gift from God this man was, not only by his incredible scholarship and voracious reading, but also in his spiritual experience.

Early experience of the mystery of God made Bede Griffiths a marked man. Clearly, his vocation could be seen at this early age as God prepared him to lead us on the pathways of God's own wisdom. The scholar, student, and mystic searcher was drawn powerfully by a desire for God. It was a passion that drew him in the tradition of all the great mystics of the past.

The writings of the early Christian spiritual writers, including Origen and the Cappadocian Fathers, speak of the longing of "eros" to a "gnosis" of God. Their theoretical speculation is incarnated in the witness of Father Bede's life. It was a deep and direct experience of God, combined with an intellectual rigor and honesty. Such a thirst for truth drew Bede to drink deeply from the wisdom of our ancient spiritual tradition, to taste the sweetness of scripture, and to be molded and inebriated by the sacraments, all set within the context of a community of faith. Yet this was not enough. In 1955 Father Bede had established himself as a Benedictine monk of great promise and a highly respected scholar. As prior of Farnborough Abbey in England, he had a very prestigious position in the Catholic Church. But the desire for Divine truth, the all-pervading longing for union with God, drew him to forsake all this respectability and, at almost fifty years old, to travel to India.

Perhaps there is another affinity: Both Bede and I left our country of birth even if for radically different reasons. But the affinity comes alive again in the fact that the move to the United States of America put me on the doorstep of Osage Monastery founded by Sister Pascaline Coff, OSB. I cannot believe my good fortune at coming to Tulsa so close to an ashram founded under the inspiration of, and with the same principles as, Father Bede's in India. Neither can I begin to tell you the profound way in which Osage Monastery has influenced my life. Through the community, guests, and visitors, the richness of Bede's own experience has touched my life. When I first encountered O+M, I had not experienced anything of the non-Christian Eastern religious tradition, and my initial reactions were not entirely positive. Little did I know how much the whole experience was to deepen and enrich my own spirituality. My awareness of the contemplative tradition in the Christian Church has been deepened and kindled into a "living flame of love" in my heart. Ultimately, I owe a debt of gratitude to Father Bede for that.

Thus far, I have spoken about the indirect way in which Bede has influenced me. Although this is really significant over a considerable period of time, nothing can express the impression made on me by meeting Father Bede first in 1990 on his visit to O+M. Nothing I had read or heard about him prepared me for that first encounter.

At the first instant, I knew I was in the presence of a holy man. The eyes are said to be "the window of the soul." Father Bede's eyes were unabashedly open and frank; they looked deep into one's own being while hiding nothing of the inner integrity of their owner. They penetrated deep, not with an uncomfortable judgment, but with a gentle acceptance and love. The body was thin and fragile, and yet in its weakness it seemed strangely invincible. The soft touch of the hand, the bow in greeting, the softness of voice, spoke in a way that a thousand volumes could not of the transforming power of the Holy Spirit. Many of the early church writers spoke of the "divinization" of the human person. In Father Bede, I felt touched by the Divine. His presence spoke eloquently of the possibility of this divinization that until meeting Bede had been but a theoretical possibility. The memory of sitting at Bede's feet, of concelebrating Holy Eucharist with him, will last forever.

When Father Bede died, it was a sad loss of someone whom I held very dear. I can only say that his departure to heaven took something of me with him. We continue to be united.

Sr. Marie Louise, Mother Superior, Ananda Ashram:

I met Father Bede for the first time in 1969. He was giving a talk to the clergy at Bishop's House, in Salem. I had been there because we were invited, but to tell you the truth, I was not impressed. Father Bede then was at least twenty-one years younger than today, and he had this short monk's hair.

I saw him again in 1975. There was a vast difference. He now had his long hair. He looked something like the prophet Isaiah, breathing wisdom, equanimity, harmony, openness, and a capacity of embracing all at one time. But I must tell you the truth that Father Bede is not a guru. He is recognized by all as guru, but I've always been telling and reminding myself that he's not a guru. He is a prophet, born in the West, shining in the East. Over the years, I have been observing him, serving him, listening to him, loving him, enjoying him — and never get tired. It is always fresh.

People keep asking me, "Tell me, Sister Marie Louise, what is it which fascinates you about Father Bede?" The answer is very simple: It is the wisdom of the man. It is not only the wisdom of the East or of the West. It is the global wisdom. East, West, put together; and the balance of the two must be fantastic.

Father Bede had his famous attack in 1990. We almost lost him. When he recovered fully, we began to notice some profound changes in Father Bede. Physically, there was no change in the man, but mystically, intellectually, spiritually, he has been embellished. The word "grown" is not enough. Embellished. *Embellished.* He is now a solid seat of wisdom. A solid authority on any belief that takes you right to the source. It is not important which direction you take, but it is the source that you reach which is important. He is an authority on every one of these directions, without discrimination. He is the lamp or the beacon that shines and sheds its light to the innumerable wayward or lost pilgrims from any country, any creed, any caste. He can relate to the savant, the scholar, the intellectual, and he can also relate to the peasant. He can relate to the high, and he can relate to the lowly. He is present, he is with this presence fully. And yet he is absent. He is fully with us and not with us.

143

For me, Father Bede is the summer of Shantivanam. The founder was the winter, the cofounder was the spring.

Father Christudas, Administrator, Saccidananda Ashram, and assistant to Father Bede for over twenty-five years:

I am forty-four years old now and have spent the last twenty-five years with Father Bede. According to my observation, I have never seen a man like him, either here in India or abroad. He doesn't have any worry. I believe and I trust that he is a sage. All through our time together, we used to quarrel constantly about problems in the ashram. I often had trouble trusting some of our guests. I used to quarrel with him just like a child. He would say, "Christudas, one thing you must understand is that everybody is important. Someone may be ninety-nine percent hopeless, but the other one percent is also created by God, as an image of God. You must accept this."

I never found such a holy man, without need for money or power or sex or whatever. He is beyond all this. Sometimes I used to ask like a friend, "Father, don't you have any sexual problems or anything like that?" He would say, "We must go beyond."

I used to say, "Father, you are too accepting." Sometimes I used to laugh at him and say, "You are not meant for this world because you are not practical at all, Father. You can't live in the world. You are beyond. So you have to stay living in the kingdom of heaven, not on earth." Then he would laugh at me.

He is a man of God, not only from his personality or intellect. What he says, he lives. What he speaks, he lives; and each and every iota of his word he keeps in his life. This is important. I have never seen such a man. I feel to follow him is a little tough. He is a man of such humility and utter sim- plicity. I firmly believe that he is a saint. I think he will be a saint. He accepts all religions, all kinds of people, even beg- gars. Everybody here feels this, even those who don't know the language. They used to go and just get a blessing. They feel at home, so such a character is very important for me.

I have never seen a man like Bede.

Appendix

History and Interpretation
of the Bible

THE BIBLE, of course, consists of the sacred book of the Jews, the Old Testament, as we call it, and the New Testament book of the Christians. As far as we can estimate, Israel came into being about 1800 B.C. Abraham is usually dated about 1800 B.C., which is also generally said to be the time of the *Vedas*. The second millennium was the time of awakening in India and in Israel.

These small tribes had their local God and, as we all know, they came into Palestine and went down into Egypt. They stayed there for two or three hundred years and then came back and settled in Palestine.

Under David, the whole nation was united in about 1000 B.C., and Solomon built the temple. Once you have a temple and a priesthood, you have leisure for writing and for history, and so the Bible began to come into being about 900 B.C.

It is usually recorded that the earliest biblical writer wrote

This is an edited version of Father Bede's last public lecture — recorded on Sunday, December 13, 1992, at Saccidananda Ashram, India. It is important to note that these are Bede's personal reflections and not intended by Bede as a scholarly presentation or commentary on current Catholic biblical scholarship.

or spoke of God under the name of "Yahweh," which means "He who is," probably in the ninth century B.C. in northern Israel. And this writer was very primitive: He speaks of God walking in the garden, taking some mud, and making Adam into a man and breathing into his nostrils and then taking Eve out of his side. This is a very anthropomorphic God.

Then, probably in the eighth century B.C., another writer took the name of *Elohim* for God. *El* is single, *Elohim* is plural. It's very interesting that the name for God in the Bible is plural. And it sometimes means the Gods, as we read in the psalm: "Thou has made man a little lower than the Elohim." Sometimes it can mean the angels. When the witch of Endor brought up Samuel from the dead of "soil," he said, "I see an *Elohim* coming out of the earth." These were divine beings, and the term *Elohim* was a commonly used one.

The word "El" is the name for God in all that region, which includes the Canaans and Semitic people. And there would be many "Els," many Gods. This type of God is very much like a Deva in India.

In the Book of Genesis Jacob dreams he sees the ladder going up to heaven. So surely God was in that place. And he calls in "Beth-el," the House of *El,* of God. On another occasion he speaks of *El Roeh,* a God who sees. So this God is manifested in different places and times.

Perhaps most important of all, there was El Eliong. This name was used in all that region for "Most High God." You may remember Melchizedek, who was the priest of El Elyon — the Most High God. He meets Abraham, and they greet each other and recognize each other. So at that stage Israel recognized the high god of the Canaanite people as one with their God. Later, of course, they rejected him altogether and took their God alone. But that was a time when it was still accepted.

Under Moses, this Elohim, with its rather general meaning — "the divine" — was given a specific name: Yahweh. And from then on, one could worship God under no other name but Yahweh, "He who is." And so Israel's religion developed in that way, and continued on with development of the law and the prophets.

Now here is the problem. Until the eighteenth century the Bible was considered to be strictly the Word of God. Every word of the Bible was taken to be divinely inspired, and so the fathers understood the Bible in an extremely sacramental and mystical sense. The most important early authority was Origen, a great master of the third century. He had studied under Ammonius Saccas, who was the leader of the School of Alexandria, where Plotinus, the great Greek philosopher, had also studied. They were contemporaries. Origen became master of the Bible, spending his whole life studying the texts. It is said he went around with a sort of truckload, or carts, full of books and papers commenting on the books of the Bible. His whole life was immersed in the Bible. And it is to him that we owe the exegesis of the Bible.

❖

It is very important to note that there were four senses of the Bible. The first was the *literal*. That is what the text is literally supposed to mean, and it was generally accepted as fundamental. But, of course, knowledge of the literal sense was often minimal. People had no idea what the text *really* meant, and so it was often badly translated. The Old Testament was written in Hebrew and the New Testament in Greek. And since the literal sense was frequently misunderstood, often little attention was paid to it.

The next sense was the *moral* sense. This involves reading the Bible to learn how to be a good Jew or a good Christian or a good human being. There was a moral law in the Bible — and that was extremely important. The classic example is Saint Gregory the Great's *Morals on the Book of Job*. Sometimes, though, the morals that were drawn from these biblical scenes are unrecognizable [in the text]. They can be beautiful and very meaningful, but often have no relation to the story.

The third sense was the *allegorical,* which involved reading the Old Testament in the light of Christ. That was the tradition of the Church right from the time of the apostles: to read the Old Testament in the light of Christ.

When Isaiah says, "The maiden shall be with child, bear a son," we immediately see this was a prophecy of the Virgin Mary bearing Jesus. The classic example of this interpretation [in the light of Christ] is Saint Augustine on the psalms — a wonderful, mystical interpretation of the psalms. For Augustine, the psalms are spoken in the name of Christ. Sometimes it's just the Divinity, but more commonly it is Christ as head of his mystical body, suffering in his mystical body. So readers are given a wonderful interpretation — but again, one that is often extremely remote from the literal sense. This allegorical approach was used by the Church for centuries.

The fourth meaning was *anagogical,* as it was called, and compared the things on earth with the things in heaven

151

above. Jerusalem, for instance, is the earthly city; allegorically it represents the Church [and individual souls], and anagogically it represented heaven, the eternal life.

So there was a wonderful development of a mystical doctrine in the Bible, from the time of Origen, to Augustine in the fourth century, right up until the seventeenth century. This development was considered normal. Saint Thomas Aquinas — as other theologians — simply accepted it.

As I just pointed out, the Old Testament was written in Hebrew. Jews spoke Hebrew until their exile in 500 B.C. Toward the end of their captivity in Babylon, when they came back to Palestine, they began speaking Aramaic, which was a similar dialect and which later became a form of Syriac.

It's quite interesting that when Jesus was in synagogue, the Bible would be read in Hebrew but commented on in Aramaic. These Aramaic commentaries on the Bible eventually became known as the Talmud. So that is how Israel developed its understanding of the Bible.

❖

As I have also mentioned, the New Testament was written in Greek — which is very important, as Jesus spoke in Aramaic. Since Aramaic was spoken all around that area of Palestine, Jesus would have learned Aramaic as a child. He might also have learned Hebrew — he probably did — in order to study the Old Testament; but he would have spoken Aramaic.

Nothing that Jesus spoke has survived, except perhaps a half-dozen words. When he raised a little girl who was supposed to be dead, he said, *Talitha cum* — Aramaic for "Little girl, arise." So a few little phrases survive, but all the rest of his teaching has been lost. We don't have a word that Jesus said, apart from those few.

His teaching and his story were then handed down in the churches, from apparently A.D. 30 to A.D. 60. As the gospels spread out of Palestine to the Greco-Roman world, they were translated into Greek. Gradually, from A.D. 60 to 90, after the apostles had passed away, there was need for a record. Hence the New Testament — written in Greek and based on the traditions that came down in the churches, from the Aramaic to the Greek translation, edited and interpreted by the different Gospel writers. So the story was put together in somewhat different ways by the different evangelists, each rendering the teaching as he understood it. Each interpretation was based in the context of the writer's own community — his own church, so to speak. So each one differs. Matthew's Gospel, for instance, is believed by some to have been originally written in Aramaic, in a Jewish setting, but edited and translated into Greek around A.D. 80. It is nearer to the Aramaic than the others. For example, whereas Mark and Luke speak of the "kingdom of God," Matthew speaks of the "kingdom of heaven," because the Jews didn't like to use the name of God — it was so sacred. Little things like that show Matthew's Gospel reflects a very Jewish background.

The Gospel of Mark was probably written in Rome, a little earlier — perhaps A.D. 70. And it is much more universal. It is written in Greek, of course, within a Hellenistic milieu, the Roman Empire, and was written for the people in general. At the time Luke was probably a Greek-speaking convert. His Greek is much more professional [than other

153

Gospel writers], and he writes very well and very beautifully. Some of the best stories of all are found in Luke.

Finally comes the Gospel of John, around A.D. 90 to 100, right at the end of the century. It is written from Ephesus, probably not by the apostle John — almost certainly not. Like all the gospels, it draws from the writer's community. Each gospel probably did derive in some way from the apostle, but John's has been developed by an extraordinary genius, because Ephesus was the center of Gnosticism. And this gnosis probably came from India (it's the same as *jnana,* the divine knowledge). John interprets the life of Jesus in the context of this divine wisdom. He says the Gospel of Matthew begins with Abraham, as the Gospel of John begins with the *Logos,* the Word of God. This is a Greek word signifying the reason of the universe.

John's Gospel moves us right out of the Jewish world into the universal world, so it's an extremely important book. Plus it covers the whole life of Jesus and more, in terms of wisdom. All in symbolic terms. Everything Jesus does here [in John's Gospel] is considered symbolic. There's always a deeper meaning behind it. So John carries the gospel beyond Palestine, beyond the limits of Judaism, and opens it up to more universal wisdom. That's why it's a climax, really, of the four gospels.

❖

The tradition of the early Church held that the Old Testament was the Word of God. Having very little of a critical sense, they [the early Christian writers] attributed the whole of the Pentateuch — the five books of the law — to Moses.

Moses wrote the books of the law; practically all the psalms were attributed to David; all the books of wisdom were attributed to Solomon; prophecies written at different times were attributed to Isaiah; and so on. It was this tradition that came down in the Church for centuries; it was the norm until the eighteenth century. Any [early] commentary was characterized by a sort of mystical sense of the Bible as the Word of God, divinely inspired, free from all error, and the model for every Christian life.

The eighteenth century marked the beginning of the critical study of the Bible. It was Richard Seymour, I believe — a Catholic exegete from France — who was the first to undertake a critical study of the Old Testament. He was rejected probably at the time, but at least he set the ball rolling. From then on, 1750 until the present day, critical study of the Bible has continued and developed. It's been a tremendous work. David Friedrich Strauss's book, *A Life of Christ,* written around 1840, was a breakthrough. It tries to see Christ, not as a divine figure, which is the traditional view, but as it was believed the gospel itself presented him. Other critical studies followed, including the well-known *The Life of Jesus* by [Ernest] Renan [1863].

Tremendous controversy ensued because the Roman Church wanted to keep to its traditional understanding, regarding all this critical study as very dangerous and wanting to prevent people from studying it. In 1900, during the time of Pope Pius X, there was an anti-Modernist movement. The Modernists tried to interpret the gospel, as we do today, in the context of the modern world, of science, and their present understanding. And this was very much against the traditional teaching. Pius X came down on the side of the conservatives who opposed this modern interpretation. He set up a commission to study/examine/interpret the Bible in an effort to give direction to Catholic exegesis. For forty years Catholic exegetes had to abide by these rules. This is how it was when I was doing Theology. We had to accept the authorship of Moses, David, and so on (actually, since the Pentateuch records Moses' death, we were allowed to say that there were maybe one or two little interjections by others, but otherwise it was all Moses). In the end, however, Pius X's points turned out to be wrong.

In 1943 Pope Pius XII's encyclical *Divino Afflante Spiritu* gave biblical scholars the freedom for critical study of the Bible; and that was a turning point. From then on to the present day, Catholic exegesis has opened up new levels of scholarship.

The greatest Catholic exegete is Raymond Brown. He is extremely sound in every way, but he is a brilliant exponent of critical study. He taught in the Union Theological Seminary in New York, which is actually a Protestant college. Catholics and Protestants mix together now, and they differ very little indeed in their critical understanding of the Bible. This new freedom to study the Bible critically is of tremendous importance for everybody. Of course, not everybody has time or leisure to go into these studies, but we should be aware of the changes that have taken place.

❖

In the seventh century, during the time of Josiah and Jeremiah, under the influence of the prophets, Deuteronomy, the Second Law, was written. That is much more profound than the others, though it is very limited in its way. Earlier, in the sixth century, at the time of Ezekiel (the other great prophet), a writer called the Priestly Writer wrote that Ezekiel belonged to the priestly caste. So what we have is a sort of patchwork of the Yahvists, the Elohists, the Deuteronomists, and the Priestly Writer, rather than one author. The Old Testament is a work of innumerable writers over the course of several centuries.

This discovery changed our whole understanding of the Bible. It is not simply the word of God come unto Moses, final and fixed. It is a gradual evolution of religion from a very primitive state through a gradual understanding of the mystery of God and salvation. What is so interesting is that the earlier stages were kept and then rewritten in a more advanced way. We can find numerous examples of the primitive elements still in the Bible.

Some are fascinating. One I always remember is the day Yahweh met Moses and sought to kill him. Then there is the strange legend of the sons of God, the angels, having relations with mortal women and producing giants. These are fables, coming down from Israel's history. Through the centuries they were rewritten in the light of deeper knowledge.

❖

And so the Bible is a story of growth, a process of primitive, barbaric people gradually discovering God, discovering his admiration for our people, discovering his relation with the nations. We had to read it as an evolutionary process, which didn't end with the Old Testament but led on to the

New. This understanding gives us a completely different attitude to the Bible. These primitive elements were gradually superseded, and the tribal God, warring against the enemies of Israel, was eventually seen as the Creator of the world.

This God had the three characteristics of holiness. First, *sadika* — which means separate. God is separate from the world. He is beyond the world, totally transcendent. This was a great innovation: the pure transcendence of God, realized as it is in the prophets — not in India, or in Egypt, or anywhere else, really. Second, he was also just and merciful. He was just in his dealings, and he demanded justice of his followers. And that was very demanding. The ancient gods could be very easygoing, and they weren't very well behaved very often, so they allowed a great deal of freedom. And in India it is believed that the gods could do almost anything. But Yahweh was a very strict and just god, yet also a merciful God. His justice was balanced by mercy. It was a wonderful concept, but it had grave limitations. I think only today we are really realizing how serious the limitations were.

The principal one is this: All the nations surrounding Israel, the Canaanites and others, were worshiping the Mother Goddess, which was the more ancient religion. Before the worship of the Father God, the Sky God, came in, the ancient people worshiped Mother Earth, Mother Nature, the Mother Goddess. We can trace the earliest relics back to about 20,000–30,000 B.C. These are figures of a female with rather large breasts and belly. It was representative of a very earthy female religion. But it had grave problems with it, including the sacrifice of children. All sorts of problems turned the Hebrew prophets against this cosmic religion — and this has told on us ever since. True, the cosmic religion had its weaknesses and dangers; but the earth was sacred, the whole universe was sacred, marriage and the body were sacred, the female was sacred, sex energy was sacred. That sacred universe is still present in India, but was condemned by the prophets. They would have nothing to do with it. It was absolutely forbidden. And that rejection has marked Christianity ever since. We are beginning to recover that cosmic religion today — actually, we are struggling to recover it.

So we see a human growth taking place in the Bible. The problem is to learn to go beyond a masculine patriarchal God, which we've still got in Christianity. Our God is still all male — it's extraordinary, when you think of it. The Father is male, the Son is male, and even the Holy Spirit (which is neuter in Greek) is male in English. This is absurd, really. I personally feel we have to recognize the Holy Spirit as feminine. And for good reason: The word *ruah* in Hebrew is feminine. But even though it is feminine, it was not necessarily popular. The point is that it was feminine, it had a feminine element in it. Throughout the Old Testament we find that feminine aspect of God, but when the Bible spread into the Greco-Roman world, which was very patriarchal, the feminine was eliminated.

❖

Because we belong to a patriarchal religion, women have no place in the Church today. Until we go beyond mere words, there will always be conflict. We see the danger, for instance, with evangelicals who cling to the words. This causes endless conflict between individuals and groups. Going beyond the words does not mean that we must dismiss the Word.

Let me offer an example of this — one that appeals to me. Take some music, a symphony, say. If you want to know that symphony, you really have to see how every note, every theme, every melody, and every movement in the symphony is part of a whole. The only way you'll know the whole is to understand all the parts. It is said that Mozart could conceive a complete symphony in his mind — total and complete — before he wrote anything down. And that is the symphony, the whole. Each note and melody and harmony can be understood only in the light of the whole.

We can learn the same from science. All external phenomena, whatsoever, can be understood only in the context of the whole, of the universal whole. And so it is with the Bible. The words of the Bible can be understood only in the context of the Word himself. And he is beyond all words.

I think the Bible poses a challenge. It still sells millions of copies; and it can deceive people. If we just stick with the words and don't go beyond the words, we have confusion. When we read the Bible in the Spirit of God — since the Spirit enables us to read the Word — we discern the text's real meaning: its meaning for our life and for the world. But reading it on the surface only can be positively harmful and cause division.

❖

In this brief overview of the Bible's evolution, we see the knowledge of God gradually grow from a very primitive understanding to a much more profound universal understanding — albeit still with limitations, such as rejection of the feminine and of the natural order in so many ways. Still, the Church goes on interpreting the Bible, century by century. The great fathers, the mystics, and the theologians, are all engaged in interpreting the Bible, interpreting the message in the light of the present. Our challenge today is to interpret the Bible in the light of Vedanta. And there is scarcely any theologian in Europe today who has studied the Vedanta. It's an amazing thing, when you think about it. There are very learned people, such as Karl Rahner — a wonderful person and a great theologian. His insights are marvelous, but he didn't know anything about Vedanta, and he didn't know a word about Mahayana Buddhism. This is absurd, and I don't think it can go on much longer.

So today we are challenged to read the Bible in the context of Vedanta, Mahayana Buddhism, Taoism, and the Sufi mystics. That is where we are moving: toward a mystical understanding of the Bible and of the whole Christian tradition, in the context of the world as we know it and in the context of science also. Because science today is moving in exactly the same direction. I've been reading a fascinating book, *Belonging to the Universe* by Fritjof Capra, one of the leading exponents of the new science, and two monks of the new Camaldolese, Brother David [Steindl-Rast] and Brother Thomas [Matus]. It shows the new paradigm in science which is opening up the whole physical world with the presence of divine energy, energizing the whole of creation. It also shows the new paradigm in theology, where we realize theology today is a gradual unfolding of the truth. It's not something fixed in the Bible or in the church fathers or anything. The mystery is there from the beginning, and it is present in Jesus, in the flesh. But our understanding had to grow continually.

Pope John XXIII made a wonderful statement. He said, "The substance of the faith remains always the same, but the mode of its expression changes." We have to keep expressing the faith, understanding it in the new light, and expressing it in a new way. And that is always the challenge for the Church. But we always tend to run back and stick with the old-fashioned tradition, thinking that is quite enough, when actually it has lost its value.

When the Bible is interpreted with the teaching of the Church in the light of world understanding of today, people are hungry for it. They are wanting. They are looking for it. If we keep on repeating the old paradigm, which no longer resonates, which no longer has meaning for people, then they just leave the Church. They won't go to mass any more. It's happening all over Europe. So we have a real challenge — but it doesn't mean that we must be frightfully learned. It's more in the perception we have to bring to these things. When we learn to meditate, we get some spiritual perception. Then we learn to discern the meaning of the Bible, we get behind the outer forms and discover the deeper meaning.

The whole Bible grew over nearly two thousand years, as the whole Church has grown over these two thousand years and is still growing. This growing process involves allowing the Holy Spirit to open the mind to the deeper dimensions of reality, of Truth, and of the deep meaning of the Bible. So we pray that the Holy Spirit enlightens us all to receive that deeper understanding to see what God is doing to us and the world today.